A Practical Step-by-Step Guide to
GROWING & ARRANGING
FLOWERS

A Practical Step-by-Step Guide to

GROWING & ARRANGING
FLOWERS

WHITECAP BOOKS

4597
This edition published in 1996 by
Whitecap Books Ltd., 351 Lynn Avenue
North Vancouver, B.C., Canada V7J 2C4
© 1996 CLB Publishing, Godalming, Surrey, England
Printed and bound in Singapore
ISBN 1-55110-457-1

Credits
Compiled by: Ideas into Print
Flower arrangements: Jane Newdick, Gill and David Oakey
Photographs: Neil Sutherland
Typesetting: Ideas into Print and Ash Setting and Printing
Production Director: Gerald Hughes
Production: Ruth Arthur, Neil Randles, Paul Randles,
Janine Seddon, Karen Staff

THE PHOTOGRAPHER

Neil Sutherland has more than 25 years experience in a wide range of
photographic fields, including still-life, portraiture, reportage, natural history,
cookery, landscape and travel. His work has been published in countless books
and magazines throughout the world.

Half-title page: A hand-tied bouquet of Oncidium *Golden Shower
and* Renanthera *Anne Black (both orchids), with leaves of* Crocosmia,
Polygonatum *and* Hosta.
*Title page: Rustic baskets are the perfect setting for two superb displays
of roses, and dahlias from the garden make excellent cut flowers.*
Left: Roses, Achillea *and* Lavatera *are planted together in a profusion
of color and shape in this pretty, pink-themed border.*
Right: Agrostemma, Coreopsis *and* Godetia *put on a dazzling show. You
can sow seeds directly into a border as long as it is completely weed-free.*

CONTENTS
PART ONE: GROWING FLOWERS

Above: Rudbeckia *'Goldsturm'* and Salvia farinacea *combine to make a striking display during late summer and fall.*

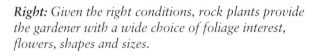

Right: Given the right conditions, rock plants provide the gardener with a wide choice of foliage interest, flowers, shapes and sizes.

Above: Nepeta mussinii *is the final plant to be added to this attractive gravel border. A wide range of plants thrive in these conditions.*

Part One

THE VALUE OF FLOWERS

Flowers are not just the window dressing of the garden; for most people, they are the single most important ingredient. Fortunately, there are plenty of them. There are flowers to grow for traditional herbaceous borders and in containers or in creative schemes, such as flower lawns and carpet bedding displays. There are flowers for cutting and flowers for extreme conditions, ranging from boggy soil through shade to hot sun. And the way to have plenty of color is to grow as many different kinds of flowers as possible - all year round.

The season starts with winter-flowering iris and hellebores, moving on to dwarf bulbs, such as snowdrops and *Iris reticulata*. These are followed by spring bedding, such as polyanthus and wallflowers, all the popular spring bulbs including daffodils and tulips, plus early-flowering perennials, such as *Brunnera* and *Pulmonaria*. Summer is no problem - annual bedding plants, roses and a huge range of herbaceous perennials take care of that. Later-flowering dahlias and chrysanthemums, Japanese anemones and *Sedum spectabile* follow on, until finally colchicums, fall crocus and kaffir lily (*Schizostylis*) join forces with fall foliage tints to bring the season to a colorful close. However, flowers alone do not make a garden. It is the way the plants are put together that makes it truly memorable. That, and the ability to pick the right flower for a given situation - and give it the right attention - this creative input is what turns a collection of flowers into a garden. This part of the book tells you how to do just that - whatever problems your garden can throw at you.

Left: The best mixed flower beds feature a variety of color, shape and height. Right: Tulips in a glazed pot.

Preparing the soil

Before planting or sowing any flowers, it is essential to get the soil in good condition. If left unimproved - hard, lumpy and short of organic matter or plant nutrients - flowers will take a long time to become established and will not grow or bloom as well as they should. Basic soil preparation involves digging, feeding and creating a fine surface ready for planting or sowing. To improve the structure and water-holding capacity of the soil, spread organic matter, such as well-rotted garden compost, manure, etc., over the soil and dig it in. This creates air spaces by 'fluffing' up the soil. Digging is traditionally done in the fall, when annual weeds and organic matter can be turned into the soil, allowing the soil bacteria to have the whole winter to 'digest' anything that is not totally decomposed. Be sure to remove perennial weeds when digging; if they are a real problem, treat them with weedkiller to eradicate them completely. If digging is not done in the fall, do it in spring, several weeks before planting, but add only very well decomposed organic matter. In spring and early summer, a few days before planting, fork the ground over roughly to loosen soil that has been flattened by winter rain, etc, and remove any weeds. Then make the final pre-planting or sowing preparations. First comes feeding. Sprinkle a general fertilizer over the ground at the manufacturer's suggested rate for pre-planting. Then rake to mix this with the soil, remove any surface stones and lumps, and produce a fine crumblike finish in which small plants and seeds can 'get away' quickly. Avoid treading on the soil again after it has been prepared.

1 Spread a layer of well-rotted organic matter (this is manure) over the soil. It should be at least 1-2in(2.5-5cm) deep.

Preparing for planting

1 When the soil has been dug over, improved and left for the winter, the next stage is to fork it over to loosen it. Break down clods by hitting them with the prongs.

2 Sprinkle fertilizer over the area, taking care to spread it evenly. Always follow the manufacturer's instructions regarding the rate at which to use the fertilizer.

3 Rake the fertilizer well into the top 1in(2.5cm) of soil. Take this opportunity to remove any small stones and other debris that have come to the surface.

4 *Sprinkle an inorganic fertilizer or an organic feed, such as fish, blood and bone, evenly over the soil at the manufacturer's suggested rate.*

2 *Dig the ground over to the full depth of the spade, turning each sod so that the organic matter is buried beneath the surface.*

3 *Rake the soil to break down clods, and remove any roots or stones, leaving it roughly level. Allow the area to lie fallow for the winter.*

Peat. Choose sphagnum moss peat for acid beds. Sedge peat has been largely superseded by cheaper, environment-friendly alternatives for general soil improvement.

Coir. Spent coir mix or natural coir (coconut fiber) is an environment-friendly alternative to peat, but expensive to use for soil improvement unless no other source of bulky organic matter is available.

Well-rotted horse manure. Useful source of bulky organic matter, but not an alternative to fertilizer. Use both.

Spent growing bag soil. After one season's use, growing tomatoes, etc., the nutrients will be exhausted but the soil is a good source of organic matter for the garden.

Fish, blood and bone fertilizer. A general-purpose organic feed for use before planting and for sprinkling between plants every 6 to 8 weeks during the growing season.

5 *Finally, rake the soil once more to mix the fertilizer into the top 1in (2.5cm) of soil and leave a fine tilth.*

Home-made garden compost. This is the result of piling damp annual weeds, grass clippings and household peelings, etc, in a compost bin for 6 to 12 months until it resembles soil.

Pea shingle. Dig in at 1-2 bucketsful per square yard/ meter to improve surface drainage of heavy clay soil. Or apply as decorative mulch.

A balanced inorganic fertilizer, one of the cheapest general-purpose feeds available. Use as described for fish, blood and bone.

1 *Prepare the ground, then trickle silver sand to mark out patterns on the soil. Mix long, narrow shapes with blocky and tapering 'teardrop' shapes for a Persian carpet-like effect.*

Sowing seeds directly in the garden

The time-saving alternative to sowing seed in pots, pricking out and then planting, is to sow straight into the garden soil. This way, there is no need to buy pots, trays or seed-sowing mixture, so it is a far cheaper way to produce plants. It is mainly used for hardy annuals, such as cornflower, clarkia, godetia, etc., as these can be sown outdoors in early spring to start flowering in early summer. Half-hardy annuals, such as French marigolds, cannot be sown outside until after the last frost and would not start flowering till the end of summer. For direct sowing, it is essential to have good, well-prepared soil that is free of weed seeds, otherwise you will not be able to tell the flowers from the weeds - they all look similar as seedlings. Two methods are used for sowing seed straight into garden soil. One is to scatter the seed over well-dug and raked soil, where you want them to flower. Seed of several different kinds of flowers can be sown in adjacent groups, marked out in advance with a trickle of sand. For this to work, you must have soil with no weed seeds whatever, which is rarely possible. The second, and better, method is to sow seeds thinly in rows in a spare patch of well-prepared soil (perhaps the vegetable garden), thin the seedlings to 1-2in(2.5-5cm) apart, then transplant them to the flower bed. The second method is also useful for sowing hardy biennials, such as wallflowers, canterbury bells and polyanthus, and herbaceous flowers (delphiniums, etc.) sown in early summer and transplanted in early fall.

2 *Sprinkle seed by hand, taking care not to overlap the edges of each shape. Adjacent patches should have contrasting colors and flower shapes, with taller kinds to the back or center.*

3 *When the whole bed has been sown, rake it very gently, barely disturbing the soil, so that you work the seeds into the surface of the soil. The sandy lines should disappear, too.*

Sowing seeds for later transplantation

1 Prepare the soil well and make a depression 0.5in(1.25cm) deep with the edge of a hoe. Sprinkle seeds thinly along it.

2 Cover the seeds with a thin scattering of soil using the rake very gently along the depression, until it is barely filled with soil particles.

3 Label the row with the name of the seed sown and date. Water well, using a fine rose, so that the soil is evenly moistened, not flooded.

4 Water the bed very thoroughly, so that the seeds and soil surrounding them are evenly damped. Use a fine rose to prevent the seed being washed away from their correct place.

Agrostemma milas

Coreopsis 'Special Mixture'

Right: Agrostemma, coreopsis *and godetia sown directly into weed-free border soil where the plants are to flower. If seedlings come up too thickly they can be thinned, but a dense stand of flowers adds to the whole effect.*

Godetia 'Sybil Sherwood'

19

1 *Slightly overfill the tray with loose seed-sowing mixture and strike the excess off level with a flat piece of wood, leaving the surface roughly level.*

A peat-based mix is fine for raising these seeds.

Raising seed in trays

If you need many plants of the same type, it pays to sow a whole packet of seed into a tray, as this will produce enough seedlings to prick out four to six trays of plants. If you share the job of plant raising with friends or neighbors and swap your spare trays of plants, it saves everyone buying several packets of seed - a good idea when you consider that flower seed germinates best in the year you buy it. Sow seeds as thinly and evenly as possible - imagine each seed turning into a small plant - and prick out the seedlings as soon as they are large enough to handle. If you are sowing medium to large flower seeds, you can avoid the job of pricking out seedlings altogether by sowing directly into small individual containers, such as 2in(5cm) pots or 'cells' (small honeycomb-like modules). Since only about 50% of flower seeds germinate, sow two medium-sized or one large seed per small container, to allow for failures. As the volume of potting mixture is so small in these tiny 'cells' they dry out very quickly, so regular watering is vital. Standing them on damp capillary matting on a greenhouse bench helps. Young plants are ready for planting out when the containers are completely filled with roots. To remove them from their 'cells', water them the day before so that the seed mix is just firm, and lift them out with a small pickle fork.

2 *Lightly firm the surface with the base of a clean flowerpot or wooden 'presser'. Leave the mixture level and about 0.25in(6mm) below the rim.*

3 *Tip the seeds into a piece of folded paper. To sow them, tap the paper gently, so that the seed is thinly and evenly distributed over the surface of the seed-sowing mixture. These are Nigella, or love-in-a-mist.*

4 *Cover the seeds to their own depth with more of the same seed mixture. Use a kitchen sieve to ensure an even covering of fine material free from lumps.*

Sowing large seeds in small pots

1 *You can sow large nasturtium seeds singly into small pots. Fill each pot with seed-sowing mix and press one seed into the middle.*

2 *This avoids pricking out, as each plant is self-contained in its own pot. When the pots are filled with root, plant them out.*

5 *Label the tray with the plant name and date. Water the seed tray by standing it in a dish of tepid water. When the surface of the seed mix turns a darker color, you know that it is wet right through.*

6 *Remove the seed tray from the water and cover it with a transparent lid. If you do not have a lid, slip the tray into a large, clear plastic bag with a couple of short sticks inside to lift the plastic up like a tent.*

Medium seeds in cells

1 *To fill the cells, pile seed-sowing mix loosely on top of the module and smooth it out evenly, making sure the cells around the edge are well filled.*

2 *Make a shallow depression in the middle of each cell and drop in two seeds. Sow only as many of one variety as you need plants, plus a few spare seeds.*

These are the seeds of Convolvulus.

3 *Cover the seeds by sieving enough seed mix over the cells to fill the depressions and bury the seed with roughly their own depth of mix.*

4 *Water well in with a fine rose on a watering can. This also helps to firm the soil. If you need to move the tray, slide a sheet of thin board under the cells.*

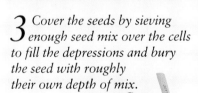

5 *Do not expect total germination; in many cases, only one of the two seeds will come up. Thin out any 'doubles' to leave only the strongest seedling.*

1 *Fill clean 3.5in(9cm) pots with seed-sowing mixture. Tip the seeds (these are French marigold) into a fold of paper and scatter thinly over the surface.*

Raising seed in pots

Although garden centers offer quite a good selection of flowers in bloom and ready to plant, it is much more satisfying to grow your own right from the start. Mail-order seed catalogs offer a far larger range of flower varieties to grow at home, including unusual ones that you may not be able to buy as plants. And, particularly if you want many plants of the same kind, raising your own can be far cheaper. Some kinds of flowers can be sown straight into the garden (see page 18), but half-hardy annuals must be sown early on in reasonable warmth if they are be in flower by the start of summer. Sow these in pots under controlled conditions. If you intend raising many plants, it is best to use an electrically heated propagator inside a frost-free greenhouse. This way you not only have the means of maintaining the right temperature for the seeds to germinate (60-75°F/15-24°C depending on the type), but you will also have room to grow them on when the seedlings are pricked out into trays. If you only need a few plants, then use warm windowsills around the house. Choose shady sills for pots of seed that are germinating, as direct sun can harm them. Then when the seedlings are pricked out, move them to a brighter spot after a few days so that they do not become drawn up and spindly. If space is short and you only need a few plants of each kind, it is not essential to prick seedlings out into trays at all - instead just plant them straight into small pots - these are likely to fit better onto a windowsill.

2 *If the seeds are very fine, sprinkle a thin layer of vermiculite over the surface before sowing them.*

3 *Tip the fine seed (here petunia) into a fold of paper and scatter it thinly and evenly over the vermiculite. Seeds fall between the particles and do not need covering.*

4 *Cover medium-sized and large seeds to their own depth with sieved seed mix. Use a clean flowerpot with small holes in the base if you do not have a sieve.*

5 *Stand the pots in a dish containing a few inches of tepid water until the surface of the soil turns dark, showing that it is wet right through.*

The plastic bag helps to create a humid atmosphere.

6 Put the pots into individual clear plastic bags and secure them with rubber bands. Place on a warm windowsill (about 70°F/21°C)) in good light but out of direct sun.

Right: *French marigolds are robust and long-flowering. Plant them out when they are already starting to bloom. Deadhead regularly.*

Below: *Petunias have large, fragile blooms that need a well-sheltered spot to keep them looking their best, especially if grown in a tall container.*

Removing seedlings

Prick out seedlings while they are tiny to give them more space to develop. Water the pot well the day beforehand. The seedlings in this pot are petunias

1 Use a dibble, the tip of a pencil or a similar implement to 'tease' the seedlings gently apart. This becomes harder to do without damage if the seedlings are left in the pot too long.

2 Hold the seedlings by a leaf, not the stem, as you transfer them to a clean tray filled with fresh seed potting mixture. Use a dibble to make holes in the mix.

3 Lower individual seedlings into the evenly spaced prepared holes until the bottom leaves lie just above surface of the soil. Gently firm the roots in with the dibble.

4 When the whole tray has been filled with seedlings, water them in using a fine rose on a watering can. Water again when necessary; keep the soil moist but not overwatered.

Instant gardening using annuals

For instant color almost anywhere, annuals are the answer. They are the simple solution for the new homeowner who wants a garden in a hurry, or for making an existing garden look its best for a special occasion. They are good for filling odd gaps in a border, for planting up containers and perfect for a balcony, patio or pathway. Annuals can also be used creatively in traditional knot gardens - or for Victorian-style carpet bedding schemes now enjoying a revival. They are also good value for planting in beds of their own where you need a splash of color that will last all summer. Use annuals in informal 'random-look' cottage-style planting schemes, or in formal beds edged with straight rows of flowers and blocks of color broken up by occasional 'dot' plants - perhaps standard fuchsias. However, annual beds are a lot of work, so do not take on more than you can comfortably manage. Plants can be grown from seed on warm windowsills indoors, or bought ready to plant from garden centers in early summer, just as they are coming into flower. Do not plant them out until after the last frost. Annuals need good soil and a sunny situation with reasonable shelter to do well. To keep plants flowering continuously they need frequent attention - watering, feeding and deadheading regularly. Since the plants do not survive freezing, pull them out in the fall and replace them with spring bulbs or winter and early spring bedding, to avoid leaving the beds empty.

Above: Use annuals to fill a narrow bed that would soon be overcrowded if planted with perennials. These are antirrhinums, tuberous begonias, lobelia and dwarf African marigolds.

Right: A colorful knot garden using Impatiens *to fill in the intricate patterns created by dwarf box hedges; A useful scheme for a shady spot as both kinds of plants are shade-tolerant.*

Annuals in containers

Tubs, troughs and hanging baskets are the perfect way of decorating a patio and for adding eye-catching detail to special places all around the garden. Favorite plants include pelargoniums, fuchsias, begonias and lobelias, but almost any compact or trailing annual is suitable. Most annuals are sun lovers and need direct sun for at least half the day. Begonia semperflorens, Impatiens and fuchsias will flower in light shade if they are in flower when planted. The best time to plant up containers is in early summer, just after the last frost. Fill the pots with any good potting mix, remove the plants from their containers and plant them close together so that the pots look well filled from the start. Containers need daily watering; allow the potting mix to take up as much water as it can.

Right: A pot of Begonia semperflorens *will be a blaze of color all summer. It can be easily moved to different spots and looks good on an outdoor table, too.*

Below: *Large containers suit a bold, mixed planting scheme. Here, verbena, pelargoniums and African marigolds make a striking and colorful display.*

Above: *Hardy annuals (Nigella, Calendula marigolds and cornflowers) grown by the 'sow where they are to grow' method, make a distinct pattern in the floral carpet covering the bed.*

Planting a perennial

1 Prepare the soil over the entire bed some time in advance of planting. Dig a hole for each plant about twice the size of its rootball.

2 Put the excavated soil next to the hole, ready for filling in around the roots once the plant is in place.

3 Put a spadeful of well-rotted manure or other organic matter in the hole and mix well. Add more manure to the excavated soil.

Perennial plants will stay in the same ground for two to four years, so it is vital to spend time on soil preparation before planting. Tackle soil pests with a soil insecticide or dig the ground several times in winter to expose pests to the birds. Dig in as much bulky organic matter as possible, sprinkle a general fertilizer evenly over the soil and rake it in shortly before planting. Perennial plants are traditionally planted in fall or early spring, but since they are dormant at that time, you may prefer to delay planting until mid-spring when some growth is visible. Buying pot-grown plants enables you to add new plants in summer when they are in full flower, but they will need generous watering during dry spells for the rest of that season to allow the roots to establish. Herbaceous perennials spread to form dense, congested clumps, with unproductive old material in the center and young flowering shoots only around the edge. After two to four years, split up the clump and throw away all the old exhausted central parts, leaving only young material, divided into fist-sized sections, to be replanted. The best time to do this is in early spring, just before the new flush of growth starts. A few of the more rugged types, such as michaelmas daisies, can be divided in the fall when the last flowers are over, but bearded irises need to be lifted and divided in summer, about six weeks after the flowers are over. Take this opportunity to improve the soil again before replanting and be sure to replant the clumps at the same depth as before. This is important: herbaceous peonies, for example, will not flower if their crown is planted more than 1in(2.5cm) below the soil surface, and bearded iris need planting so that the top half of each horizontal rhizome is above ground or they will suffer from the same problem.

4 Sprinkle a handful of general purpose fertilizer into the hole and mix well with the soil. Add half a handful of fertilizer to the pile of soil alongside the hole and, again, mix well.

5 *Tip the plant gently out of its pot (knock the base of the pot sharply against something solid if the plant is difficult to dislodge). Slide the plant out without breaking up the rootball.*

6 *Lift the plant by its rootball into the hole. Do not handle the plant by its stems. The top of the rootball should lie roughly level with the soil surface. Rotate the plant until its best side faces the front of the bed.*

7 *Surround the rootball with the improved soil excavated from the planting hole, and firm it lightly down. Add more soil to bring it up to the level of the surrounding bed.*

8 *Water well in, trickling water around the edge of the rootball. Mulch with 1-2in (2.5-5cm) of rotted organic matter or bark chips and keep well watered.*

Traditional herbaceous borders

The traditional English country house herbaceous border is long and narrow and backed by a yew hedge that provides a green background. The border is generously filled with a wide selection of flower shapes, sizes and colors, all apparently randomly mixed. (In fact, it needs careful planning to ensure that contrasting shapes are put next to each other and that colors are evenly distributed throughout the bed.) Since only herbaceous plants are used, the border looks bare in winter, but by choosing plants carefully it is possible for a big border to look good from spring to the fall. (If the border is small, aim for midsummer interest mainly, to avoid seasonal gaps.) Although the effect is stunning, a traditional herbaceous border takes a lot of looking after. Tall plants such as delphiniums must be staked, as the hedge creates shade that draws plants up, causing weak stems. The hedge also harbors weeds, pests and diseases, as well as taking moisture out of the soil, so the flowers need spraying, generous mulching and frequent hoeing for good results. The hedge also needs clipping. Yew only needs cutting once a year, so this can be done before the border grows up. However, a faster growing hedge needs cutting several times during the season. In this case, leave an access path at least three feet wide (about 1m) between the hedge and the back of the border. If space allows, it is not a bad idea to leave room for a path anyway, as this makes routine work like mulching, hoeing and weeding much easier as you can reach into the bed from both sides without treading on the soil.

Above: *A traditional mixed border, with a clipped conifer hedge forming a leafy backdrop, and a profusion of perennials growing in amongst each other in a wild mixture of colors.*

Left: *Lupins bloom in early summer. Cut them down hard after flowering as they sometimes produce a second flush of flowers. They need sunny, well-drained soil.*

Island beds

An island bed is an informal-shaped bed cut into the lawn where you can walk right round it. It can be any shape you like; have one large bed or make a group of several smaller ones. Island beds are usually planted with the tallest plants in the middle and progressively shorter ones round the edge, so they look good from all angles. As the plants receive light from all round, their stems are stronger and need less staking. Being stronger, the plants suffer less from pests and diseases. Routine chores are easier, as you can reach plants from the lawn. Put

Below: The trick of creating an eye-catching herbaceous border is to use plenty of contrasting shapes - upright spikes, flat-topped flowers and daisy shapes make a good basis.

Above: Island beds blend in well with a more informal garden.

in traditional herbaceous plants and lilies but choose compact modern varieties. Or try using ornamental grasses and summer flowering bulbs.

Below: Equally traditional is the double fronted border, which has a path between two borders face to face. These often have a seat or statue at the end as a focal point.

Planning a spring border

After a long dull winter, the first spring flowers are always welcome, but instead of just dotting them around the garden, make them into more of a spectacle by concentrating them together in a spring border. This does not have to be an isolated feature that looks dull for the rest of the year - spring plants can be happily integrated into a summer border, where they provide the starting point for a long season of color. Plan the border so that there is a good balance between spring and summer flowers - the foliage of spring flowers will provide a leafy 'foil' for those that follow on later. Plant tall summer flowers, such as delphiniums, towards the back of the border; spring kinds tend to be low-growing, so plant them towards the front. Low bulbs, such as *Anemone blanda,* make a colorful carpet under shrubs and towards the front of the border, while taller kinds, such as daffodils, are best kept in clumps towards the middle, where the untidy foliage will be partly hidden by other plants. Buy pots of spring annuals, such as polyanthus, colored primroses and forget-me-not, already in flower, to fill any odd gaps. In a large garden where there is room, you could create a spring 'cameo' purely from early flowers, which makes a much more solid effect. It also gives you a chance to create interesting plant associations based around favorite plants, such as euphorbias, *Epimedium* and hellebores. For a specially striking yellow trio, try *Euphorbia wulfenii,* narcissi and the early yellow *Paeonia mlokosewitschii.*

Cheiranthus 'Bowles Mauve'

Dicentra formosa

Doronicum orientale *(leopard's bane)*

Dicentra spectabilis 'Alba'

Bergenia 'Ballawley'

Primula denticulata

Primula rosea 'Grandiflora'

Above: *Forget-me-nots, with bluebells, tulips,* Helleborus orientalis *and* Dicentra spectabilis 'Alba'.

Above: Daffodils and Helleborus foetidus *(stinking hellebore) make a successful plant association. Despite its name, the hellebore does not smell unpleasant unless leaves are damaged.*

Above: Paeonia mlokosewitschii *is a beautiful early-flowering species, which for obvious reasons is better known by its common name of 'Mollie the Witch'.*

Above: Euphorbia wulfenii *has striking lime green spring flowers. This is a canary yellow form of it called 'Lambrook's Gold', which must be propagated from cuttings.*

Ranunculus
(turban buttercup)

Primula
vulgaris
(cultivated
primrose)

Narcissus
'Hawera'

Primula vulgaris
flore-plena
'Dawn Ansell'

Hyacinths

Pansies

Primula rosea

Tulip 'Orange Nassau'

Viola 'Prince Henry'

The magnificent lilies

Lilies are one of the most spectacular and collectable summer-flowering bulbs. Some varieties need lime-free soil, while others do not mind. Most prefer to be grown in a border surrounded by other plants, with the bulbs shaded but their tops in sun, while others enjoy shady woodland conditions. Some lilies are good for growing in pots on a patio, but if your soil is not suitable for the species you want to grow, any lilies can be grown in large pots containing a suitable potting mixture, sunk into the ground. Full cultural details of individual varieties can be found in the catalog (if bought by mail order) or on the back of the pack (if you buy at a garden center). Although pot-grown plants are available in flower during the summer, lilies are normally bought as dry bulbs in spring. Regardless of other requirements, all lilies need good-quality, well-drained, moisture-retentive soil when grown in the garden. Add plenty of well rotted organic matter (coir is ideal) and gritty sand before planting. As an extra precaution against rotting, place a generous layer of gritty sand at the base of each planting hole. Plant the Madonna lily *(Lilium candidum)* with the tip of the bulb just showing above ground, but as a general rule, plant lily bulbs so that they are covered by twice their own depth of soil. Plant three or five lilies of the same variety together in a group, spaced 4-6in(10-15cm) apart, for a good show. Once planted, lilies need not be dug up or divided until groups are overcrowded and lack vigor. Mulch generously each spring and feed regularly during the growing season as they are heavy feeders.

Choose good-quality bulbs.

1 Assemble six bulbs, soil-based potting mix and a 14in(15.5cm) diameter pot (to allow sufficient planting depth). Half-fill the pot.

2 Place the lilies on the potting mix, spaced an equal distance apart. In pots, you can plant lilies closer together than you would in a garden.

3 Arrange five bulbs around the edge of the pot and one in the center. Cover the bulbs with potting mix; make sure that they stay upright.

4 Once it is in flower, you can stand a pot-grown lily on a patio (but make sure that the pot is in shade) or sink the pot to its rim in a border for instant color in a vacant spot.

Below: *As a general rule, plant lily bulbs so that the tip of each bulb is covered by 6in(15cm) of soil. The soil should be moisture-retentive but well-drained, and not too wet in winter.*

Above: *To plant lilies outdoors, lay the bulbs informally on the prepared soil, about 12in(30cm) apart. Dig individual holes for each bulb.*

Below: *Here lilies are planted with a cut-leaved elder and lady's mantle. Try planting them with a low foreground of shorter plants to keep bulbs cool.*

Left: *Lilies flower in summer; since their blooms are large and exotic-looking, a good leafy background shows them off to advantage. This variety is 'Journey's End'. Plant groups of different varieties for a long succession of lily flowers throughout the summer months.*

Connoisseur's flowers – something special

Given a few years growing experience, it is not unnatural to develop a particular interest in one group of plants, and to hunt out unusual, new, old or rare cultivars. Before you know it, you have started a collection. People collect all kinds of plants - hostas, old-fashioned roses, alpines, and rare hardy plants generally. Several specialist societies exist to help enthusiasts obtain and learn about choice plants. (For details of membership consult gardening magazines.) Collectables often have unique 'personalities' or cultivation requirements, and their foibles are all part of the attraction to a collector. Old roses for instance have very distinctive flowers, blowsy and often 'quartered', with a range of colors and scents often lacking in modern kinds. However, they suffer from one drawback to general gardeners, namely a very short flowering season, only six to eight weeks in early summer. One breeder of modern roses has got round this by producing New English Roses, which have the distinctive flowers of old roses combined with the long flowering season of modern kinds. These are just as easy to grow as normal roses. Some collectable plants, however, need special attention.

The reason scarce plants are in short supply is usually because they are difficult to propagate, or need very precise growing conditions and cultivation. Choice alpines, for example, are often grown in pots and protected in winter in specially constructed greenhouses or cold frames. Whole beds may be designed around a collection of one particular alpine species.

Right: *As their common name suggests, the flowers of chocolate cosmos, Cosmos atrosanguineus, have a strong scent of chocolate. The plant was saved from the brink of extinction and recently re-released. It grows to 30in(75cm) and, like a dahlia, it dies down to a tuber in winter. It is rather tender.*

Left: *Gold-laced polyanthus were 'florists flowers', bred and exhibited by 18th century flower fanciers in the UK. Once, hundreds of named varieties existed. Now only this and the silver-laced polyanthus remain, but they are still very lovely.*

Above: *Auriculas were also old 'florists flowers', although today they are again very collectable and plenty of new varieties are being bred. 'Argus' shown here was raised in 1895. Modern varieties are easier to come by and simpler to cultivate.*

Right: *Rosa Mundi (Rosa gallica versicolor)* is said to date back to the 12th century, when it was named after Henry II's mistress, the fair Rosamunde. It grows to 48x48in (120x120cm). It is easy to grow and stays fairly disease-free.

Right: Rosa chinensis mutabilis *is one of the China roses; this one has pink- or purple-tinged young foliage. Species roses of all kinds are gaining in popularity today. As they often make large prickly plants, they are good for hedging or wild gardens.*

Left: *'Graham Thomas' is one of the best New English Roses, named after one of the most influential rose experts. The plant grows to 48x48in (120x120cm) and has tea-scented flowers all summer.*

35

Charming sweet peas

Left: Sweet peas can make a striking feature, as here in a terracotta pot, with plants trained to climb up a rustic wigwam of loosely interwoven willow wands.

Sweet peas are surprisingly versatile traditional favorites. They are good both as cut flowers and garden plants. Grow them up a 'tent' of twiggy pea sticks to give height to a border, or as climbers on trellis or netting. Knee-high dwarf cultivars can be grown in hanging baskets, and as low-flowering summer 'hedges', edging lawns or borders. Any sweet peas can be cut for indoors - the more you cut, the more flowers are produced.

However, sweet peas that have been allowed to ramble freely often have short, kinked or bent stems. If you want sweet peas with long straight stems for cutting, grow them as cordons. Here, each plant is trained individually up a cane as a single stem, secured with plant rings or raffia. Nip out the thin curly tendrils between thumb and finger, otherwise they 'grab' hold of the flower stems, making them kink. Seed catalogs list a huge range of different named varieties of sweet peas and mixtures are also available. Not all varieties are well perfumed, so check the descriptions. Old-fashioned cultivars, such as 'Painted Lady' and the various old-fashioned mixtures that are sometimes available, are best in this respect. Their flowers are not as large as in the modern, wavy-edged, Spencer types, but their scent makes up for it. Even if you do not cut sweet peas for the house, remove deadheads at least once a week, otherwise the plants quickly stop flowering.

1 *Sow sweet pea seeds spaced 1.5in (3.75cm) square in a tray filled with seed sowing mixture. You can sow the seeds in early fall for early flowers, but spring is the usual time for sowing them.*

2 *Push each seed into the sowing mixture until it just disappears below the surface. The seeds should be buried to their own depth in the sowing mixture.*

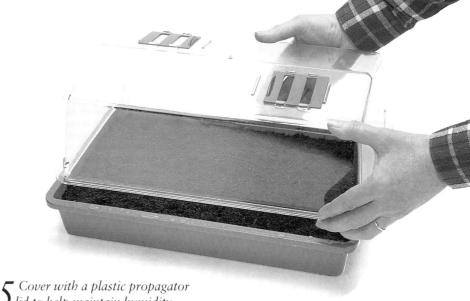

3 *Pinch the sowing mix together over the top of each seed to fill the hole. If necessary, sprinkle a fine layer of extra sowing mix over the surface.*

4 *Water thoroughly and let surplus moisture drain away. Large seeds absorb a great deal of water before germinating so check the soil regularly.*

5 *Cover with a plastic propagator lid to help maintain humidity during germination. When the first shoots appear, slide back the vents.*

Above: *A flowering sweet pea hedge, produced by spacing plants about 12in(30cm) apart and training them up a post and netting fence. Regular cutting encourages new buds.*

Left: *Sweet peas hold themselves up to trellis or netting using their tendrils, but these also tangle together and catch on neighboring flower stems, making them bend or kink.*

6 *Remove the lid entirely when the shoots are 1in(2.5cm) high. Gradually acclimatize the plants to harder conditions by standing them outside when the weather is fine.*

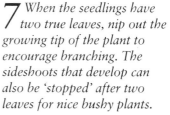

You can easily remove the growing tip by nipping it out between thumb and forefinger.

7 *When the seedlings have two true leaves, nip out the growing tip of the plant to encourage branching. The sideshoots that develop can also be 'stopped' after two leaves for nice bushy plants.*

37

Tuberous begonias in tubs

Tuberous begonias are very useful flowers all around the house and garden. Use them on windowsills, in sunrooms, porches or a greenhouse, and outdoors in containers or beds. There are various types: the normal, upright-growing, double-flowered plant in a range of colors; trailing begonias for hanging baskets; and cultivars with unusual flower forms, such as anemone-centered, semi-double or frilled-edged. The very large-flowered kinds are intended for exhibition and need greenhouse cultivation. In spring, you can buy dry, dormant begonia tubers, which are easy to grow. Established plants in pots are also available all summer. However, the cheapest way to acquire a good collection is to grow your own from seed. Sprinkle the dustlike seed thinly on the surface of finely sifted seed mixture, and cover the pot with plastic film. Stand the pot in a dish of tepid water until it is completely moist. Keep it in a warm place at a steady temperature and out of direct sunlight. When the seedlings are large enough, prick them out individually into a tray of similar seed mix, and cover them with a plastic propagator lid to retain humidity. Finally, pot the seedlings individually into small pots. Expect seed-raised plants to start flowering in their second year.

Above: To produce large blooms on a tuberous begonia, nip out the two tiny buds on either side of the main flower. This variety is called 'Pin Up'.

Tuberous begonias lose their stems and leaves in the fall; when they start yellowing in late summer, reduce the feed and water until the soil in the pots is quite dry. Store the pots in a dry, frost-free place for the winter, or empty the pots and store the dry tubers in paper bags in a drawer indoors.

1 *To avoid planting begonia tubers upside down, sit the dry corms convex side up in a dish of damp seed mixture on a warm windowsill.*

2 *When fat pink buds are visible in the dished surface of the corm, you can be certain it has started to grow and is the right way up, although no roots have appeared yet. This is the right stage for potting.*

3 *To plant the corm, loosely fill a 4 or 5in(10 or 13cm) diameter pot with potting mixture to within 0.5in(1.25cm) of the rim. The potting mixture can be either peat, coir or soil-based.*

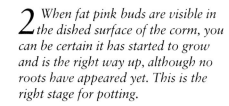

Left: *A row of similar tuberous begonias makes an attractive semi-formal feature in a terracotta trough. The effect is of a cottage windowsill. Deadhead regularly to keep new buds coming all summer.*

Right: *Trailing tuberous begonias are good for hanging baskets, here seen growing with fuchsia, lobelia, busy lizzie and petunias. Trailing begonias need not be disbudded, as they naturally have many smaller flowers.*

5 The end result: a well-grown begonia plant with perfect blooms the size of tea cups that make a stunning display in their container.

Right: *Once the plant is coming into flower, you can transfer it to a larger container, such as this formal outdoor urn.*

4 Press the base of the corm firmly into the center of the pot, leaving the very top of the corm just showing above the surface. Water; keep out of bright sun until growing well.

Late season border

Towards the end of the season, many herbaceous borders are looking past their best as summer flowers come to an end. But there are plenty of species that flower in late summer. By planting these among the summer-flowering kinds, the late bloomers provide foliage that acts as a foil to summer flowers, then take over the interest from them as the earlier flowers are deadheaded or cut down. (Some early summer flowers, such as delphiniums and lupins, give a second, later show if they are cut down almost to ground level as soon as the flowers are finished). To make the most of late flowers, plant tall kinds behind shorter summer flowers and make sure that all plants are given sufficiently wide spacing, otherwise it is easy to find your late crop of flowers have been smothered by earlier plants. Short late flowers, such as *Liriope muscari,* and clumps of fall bulbs, such as colchicums, are useful for planting at the front of the border to mask seasonal gaps. To make the most of a late display, do not allow your vigilance to slip in midsummer, when a border of summer flowers could safely be allowed to 'slip' a little. Make sure that you regularly deadhead the whole border and cut down early flowers to ground level when the foliage starts dying down, so that late flowers stand out against clean foliage. For much the same reasons, it is important not to get behind with routine chores, including weeding, feeding and slug control, if you want a good late show from your border. And have a few pots of late-sown annuals (sown thinly in pots in early summer and planted out in a clump) ready to tuck into any bare gaps for an instant show of color.

Left: Purples, mauves, oranges and yellows are the colors that dominate a late border. Here, they are provided by Sedum spectabile, Rudbeckia, Solidago (golden rod) and Michaelmas daisies.

Left: Diascia flanaganii *flowers from midsummer well into the fall. The plants make spreading carpets about 6-9in(15-23cm) high that look good contrasting with silver artemisias.*

Right: Rudbeckia '*Goldsturm*' and Salvia farinacea *both flower well through late summer and the fall, until the first serious frosts cut them back.*

Late summer flowers

Aconitum autumnale
Agapanthus *(African lily)*
Anemone japonica
Aster amellus, ericoides, novae angliae *(New England asters)*
Aster novi-belgii *(Michaelmas daisies)*, Cimicifuga *(bugbane)*
Dendranthema *(formerly* Chrysanthemum*)* rubellum *(hardy cottage chrysanthemums)*
Helianthus *(perennial sunflower)*
Heliopsis
Kniphofia '*Little Maid*' and '*Percy's Pride*', Ligularia
Liriope muscari, Penstemon
Phlox, Physalis franchetii
Phygelius, Rudbeckia fulgida
Schizostylis *(kaffir lily)*
Solidago *(golden rod)*
Tricyrtis *(toad lily)*

Keeping summer annuals in flower

Many summer annuals can be kept flowering till fall. Keep them regularly fed, never let them go short of water and nip off all the dying flowerheads as soon as you spot them. Check plants over at least once a week.

Right: *There are several named varieties of the butterfly plant,* Sedum spectabile. *All make good late-flowering plants, with the added bonus of striking foliage decorated with heads of vivid green buds earlier in the summer. Good for cutting.*

Dazzling dahlias

1 *Choose a pot large enough to take the dahlia tuber with room to spare and half fill it with potting mixture. Sit the tuber in the middle.*

2 *Cover the tuber with 2in(5cm) of potting mix, filling the pot almost to the rim. Tap the pot down sharply to consolidate the potting mix.*

3 *Water and put in a frost-free place. When the first shoots are 3-4in(7.5-10cm) tall, you can remove a few to use as cuttings if you wish.*

After a long spell out of fashion, dahlias are back in favor again. They make superb free-flowering plants for midsummer to fall displays, but their large, distinctive flowers can easily overpower more delicate neighbors, so they need placing with care. Plant them in groups among spring and early summer-flowering shrubs to brighten up the border later in the year or keep them to a bed of their own. Dahlia flowers are wonderful for cutting, and the more you pick, the more you get. Named varieties are available with flowers ranging from tiny to gigantic, and from neat pompon shapes to open-faced collarettes and spiky-petaled cactus types, in virtually every color except true blue. Dahlias are grown from tubers planted out in late spring, about two weeks before the last frost. A small selection is available in garden centers as dry tubers in spring, but enthusiasts send for catalogs from specialist nurseries or order plants at flower shows in late summer. Rooted cuttings are occasionally available in spring, but do not plant these out until after the last frost. Dahlias need moist, rich soil in a sunny spot and some regular attention for best results. Plants continue flowering right up to the first fall frosts. In mild areas with free-draining soil, some people can get away with leaving dahlia tubers in the ground over the winter, protecting the tubers under a deep layer of leaf litter. Elsewhere, lift and store them (see panel).

Right: *Compact dahlias make good plants for the front of a border, but they are also good grown in pots - try them on a patio, or plunged to their rims to fill late gaps in borders.*

Lifting and storing dahlia tubers

Leave plants in the ground until early frosts start to blacken the foliage. Cut the stems down to 6in(15cm) and dig the plants up carefully to avoid damaging the tubers. Turn them upside down so that the sap can drain out of the hollow stems. When they are completely dry, rub any soil off the tubers. Store them in a dry, frost-free shed, away from rodents. Check the tubers regularly, and if you see any rot, cut out the affected area and dust the cut surface with yellow or green horticultural sulfur.

1 To grow dahlias in a border, dig a hole into well-prepared soil, about 8in(20cm) deep and wide enough to take the tuber with space to spare.

2 Place the tuber on top of a small mound of soil in the bottom of the hole, and space the roots out so that they make good contact with the soil.

3 Hammer in a strong stake just behind the tuber. If you leave this till later you risk damaging the tuber. Cover the tuber and fill the hole.

Above: The tip of the tuber should be 6in(15cm) below the ground. If a late frost threatens the first shoots, cover them with bracken or peat.

Right: Dahlias make good cut flowers. Shake them lightly to dislodge any earwigs and put the stems into water immediately after cutting them.

Cut dahlias when there are plenty of tight petals in the center of the bloom for longest vase life. Stand them in deep tepid water.

Cactus-flowered dahlias are characterized by quilted petals.

Remove lower leaves before arranging or they make the water slimy.

Top up the water in vases daily, as dahlias are heavy drinkers.

Cottage garden borders

Nowadays, many people with modern houses have a cottage garden. The popular 'recipe' includes roses round the door, hollyhocks at the gate, flowers mixed with vegetables, fruit trees instead of flowering shrubs, and no lawn but gravel paths edged with flowers or low lavender hedges everywhere. However, most people today want at least a small lawn, and vegetables grown amongst flowers are never as productive as when grown in rows in a proper vegetable garden. The real secret of a successful cottage garden is to have carpets of plants covering the borders so that no soil is visible, and to grow plants that look 'cottagey' even if they are not entirely authentic. Old-fashioned annuals, such as godetia, wallflowers, snapdragons, clarkia and alyssum, can be allowed to seed themselves about randomly - simply pull up any that grow where they are not wanted. Rampant spreading plants like golden rod, lemon balm *(Melissa officinalis)* and many of the herbaceous campanulas can be grouped in a bed of their own and left to fight for space. These are useful for creating a low-maintenance cottage garden, although the result can be a little on the wild side for many people's liking.

Above: A plain picket fence and old-fashioned flowers such as these snapdragons create an unsophisticated feeling of 'olde worlde' charm.

Left: When you mention cottage gardens, this is what immediately springs to mind: riotous borders overflowing with a huge mixture of flowers apparently fighting for space.

Other cottage styles

As an alternative, try beds of roses underplanted with low carpeting herbaceous flowers, with tall delphiniums, tree mallow and thalictrum growing through towards the back. Enthusiasts also find room for choice cottage 'treasures', such as gold-laced polyanthus, old-fashioned pinks and auriculas, which need special care to thrive.

Right: Many wildflowers are old cottage garden plants. Obtain seeds from specialist suppliers; do not take plants or seeds from the wild.

Popular plants for cottage gardens

Astrantia
Aquilegia
Crown imperials
Cultivated primroses
Daffodils
Forget-me-not
Hardy fuchsia
Honeysuckle
Lavender
Myrtle
Nasturtium
Pinks
Pulmonaria
Pyrethrum
Rosemary
Old-fashioned roses
Sedum acre *(stonecrop)*
Sempervivum arachnoideum
(cobwebbed houseleek)
Sweet william, Wallflowers

Above: Traditionally, the front gardens of old cottages did not have a lawn, but were completely filled with a carpet of flowers, leaving just a path to the door.

Right: Hardy cranesbills, mallows, roses and lady's mantle are all at home in a cottage garden. Rejuvenate clumps of perennial plants every few years.

Scented foliage

Herbs
Lavender
Salvia grahamii
(blackcurrant scent)
Salvia rutilans *(pineapple scent)*
Scented-leaved pelargoniums
*(various citrus, spice, balsam,
rose and pine scents)*

Below: *Herbs and roses - a cottagey combination chosen for scents and colors. The herbal scents are released when the leaves are brushed, so plant herbs towards the front of the border.*

Scented borders

Scent is one of the most overlooked assets of a flower garden, yet by choosing carefully it is possible to have a constantly changing perfumed accompaniment to a walk round the garden. Seating areas are particularly good places for perfumed plants, or they could be used as the inspiration for an entire fragrant garden. Scented plants come in two basic types; those with perfumed flowers and those with aromatic leaves. Choose some of each for a succession of scents. Flowers deliver their perfume all the time they are fully open and some, such as lilies, only last a short time. Some of the best scented flowers have the most uninteresting blooms - you would hardly notice night-scented stock and sweet rocket, so tuck them in with more spectacular but unscented displays. Modern cultivars of old scented favorites, such as flowering tobacco and many roses, have lost much of their scent - choose old-fashioned kinds where possible. Use fragrant flowers in distinct groups all round the garden, so that their scents do not overlap. Aromatic leaves need to be bruised to release their fragrance, so place them where you can brush past them. Since scent is easily dispersed on the breeze, choose a sheltered, preferably enclosed, site for scented plants. Although many plants are scented during the day, most produce their strongest scent in the evening to attract night-flying insects for pollination. Scent will also be strongest when the air is warm and humid.

Above: *Not all roses are heavily perfumed, but one of the best is this 'Fragrant Cloud', a hybrid tea. Check rose catalogs for details of other well-scented kinds.*

Scented flowers

Cosmos atrosanguineus
(chocolate-scented cosmos)
Dianthus *(pinks)*
Hesperis matronalis
(sweet rocket)
Honeysuckle, Hyacinths
Jasminum officinale *(Jasmine)*
Lavender, Lilium regale,
candidum *and some lily hybrids*
Nicotiana affinis
(flowering tobacco)
*Night-scented stock
Roses, Stocks
(Brompton or East Lothian)
Sweet peas
Wallflowers*

Above: Nicotiana alata *is well known for scenting the evening garden. Few modern varieties are strongly scented; try* 'Fragrant Cloud' *and the tall* Nicotiana sylvestris; *both white.*

Above: *Pinks and lavenders; both the foliage and flowers of lavender are scented; this cultivar is a form of French lavender with large petals,* Lavandula stoechas *'Pendunculata'*

Right: Santolina chamaecyparissus *(cotton lavender) has silvery foliage that smells attractively herbal when bruised. Victorian ladies brushed their clothes with it to repel moths.*

47

Themed borders

Above: *Yellow* Potentilla, Achillea, *hollyhock and* Helichrysum *flowers combine well with green, blue-gray, silver and cream-variegated foliage.*

Below: *This restful border features* Knautia macedonica, Lathyrus latifolius, *tree mallow,* Salvia superba, Bergenia *and* Dahlia *'Rutland Water'.*

Pastel color themes of pinks, mauves and purples have long been firm favorites in the garden, but now there is an increasing trend for much more limited color schemes. These are usually based on one color, such as white, plus every possible foliage color - variegated, gold, gray, silver, blue and every shade of green. Rather than turn an entire small garden over to such an extreme style, it is much better to make over an individual bed. And instead of using a single color, which is very difficult to do well, it is much better to use a slightly broader color scheme. A 'blue' garden could, for example, contain purple, lilac and blue flowers. This avoids the difficulty of finding enough different true blue flowers to fill the space, and the slight variation of shades adds depth and interest without straying too far from the chosen color scheme. Similarly, a 'yellow' garden could contain cream, buff-orange, and earthy ocher colors, as well as true yellows - a yellow garden looks particularly good with plenty of lime green and gold-variegated foliage added, too. Regardless of the colors you choose, the great trick is to select plants whose shape and texture contrast well together. Avoid anything bland, and go instead for spiky or strap-shaped foliage, huge architectural shapes, bold upright spires, neat hummocks, dense spreading ground cover dotted with flowers, arching stems, frothy flowers, prickles, globes and other strong shapes.

Right: *Both the flowers and leaves of* Eryngium alpinum *have harsh, spiky shapes. These are exactly the sort of striking architectural forms that are invaluable in a color schemed garden.*

Above: *Red borders are great fun though not easy to get 'right'. Here, shades of purplish-red are used throughout, with an enormous range of leaf and flower shapes and sizes.*

Right: *A cool white spring border, with three cultivars of white tulips in front of a fragrant viburnum. White pansies nestle among the foliage of variegated hostas, silver artemisia,* Stachys lanata, *green iris and box.*

1 Dig a planting hole about twice the size of the pot in which the rose is growing. The soil should be well dug over and manured.

2 Put a spadeful of well-rotted manure into the hole and mix it in with the soil, so that the rose roots grow into good, retentive soil.

3 Sprinkle a handful of general-purpose or rose fertilizer over the base of the hole; mix it well into the soil.

4 The rose should have been well watered on the previous day. Tip it carefully out of its pot without breaking up the ball of roots.

Container roses

Compact roses, sold under the general name of patio roses, make good plants for tubs in any sunny spot. Bush plants are most often seen, but short standards can look very effective amongst a display of shorter plants. This technique is particularly stunning when used for spreading cultivars, such as 'Nozomi', which produces a small weeping tree when grown as a standard. Miniature roses can also be grown in containers, but being slightly more tender are best moved under cover for winter in all but the mildest regions. Otherwise, overwinter potted roses by sinking the pot to its rim in vacant soil in a garden bed, or by lagging it with hessian or old newspaper. Be sure to prevent the soil in the pot from freezing solid, which damages the roots. Prune container roses in the usual way, but less severely; with miniature roses, remove any dead twigs and slightly thin out cluttered growth. Because the roots are confined in a pot, feed container roses regularly during spring and summer with a liquid rose food. Water during the growing season, but do not allow pots to become waterlogged in winter. Container roses planted in a soil-based potting mix can remain in the same pot for two to three years. Then either replant the rose into a garden bed or move it to a larger pot with fresh potting mixture in early spring.

Right: Remove the individual heads of floribunda roses, such as this 'Korresia', when they are over. Cut the whole stem back about 12in (30cm), just above a growth bud for more flowers.

5 Position the rose with its best 'side' facing out front and the top of the rootball level with the soil surface.

6 Fill in the planting hole around the rootball. Use improved topsoil made by mixing the border soil with a little more well-rotted manure and a sprinkling of fertilizer.

7 Firm the new soil lightly down. Add more soil to bring the level back flush with the surrounding area.

8 Mulch with a 2in(5cm)-deep circle of well-rotted manure. Start 2in (5cm) from the stem, extending out 18in(45cm).

9 Finally, water the plant in well, concentrating the water near the stem and around the edge of the rootball. Continue to water the rose thoroughly right through the first season whenever the soil is dry.

A rose border

Nurseries and garden centers now stock a wider selection of roses than ever. Modern bush roses flower from early summer until the fall, and include the hybrid teas and floribundas, also known as large-flowered and cluster-flowered roses. Miniature roses grow to about 12-24in(30-60cm) tall, while patio roses are about halfway in size between miniature and bush roses, and ideal for containers. Ground cover roses are prostrate, but it is difficult to weed around them, as their stems are so prickly. However, grown on upright stems as short standards, they are spectacular, creating a waterfall of flowers. Old-fashioned shrub roses are grown for their classic scent and charming old-world colors. They are bush roses but often a bit straggly and in need of support; most only flower in early summer though some kinds have occasional flowers later too. Nowadays, some modern roses, such as the New English roses) are bred to look like old roses but with the long flowering season of modern kinds - the best of both worlds. Traditionally, roses were grown in beds of their own with bare soil underneath, while modern bush roses look good grown with a carpet of annual flowers. Old-fashioned roses look best treated like any flowering shrubs and grown in a mixed border of cottage garden flowers or herbaceous plants, particularly those that flower after the roses are over.

Left: Herbs are good for the front of a border of roses where the soil gets dry. Here, 'Graham Thomas', one of the New English roses, teams effectively with the purple-leaved sage.

Left: *Standard and half-standard roses add height to a border without taking up too much space. This is Rosa 'Excelsa', a once-flowering rambler that can attain a height of 20ft(6m).*

Below: *Modern roses are all too rarely used as flowering shrubs in mixed borders. Here, 'Masquerade', a floribunda, mingles with* Campanula, Alchemilla *and other border plants.*

Left: *Arches or pillars are useful for accommodating climbing roses, such as 'Veilchenblau' and 'Compte de Chambord', shown here, and help to make the border look tall and solid.*

Below: *Miniature roses are often mistaken for houseplants, but they are outdoor varieties and require the same care as their larger cousins. This red variety is called 'Royal Baby'.*

Left: *Violets make superb ground cover under roses, as they thrive in light shade and do not compete for nutrients. This old moss rose, 'Jean Bodin', is planted with* Viola cornuta. *Violets self-seed readily, and soon create their own carpet. Plant them 1in(2.5cm) apart.*

Flowers for dry shade

Some gardens are in almost permanent shade due to the presence of large overhanging trees or nearby buildings, but even relatively normal gardens often have 'problem' corners in between walls or fences where the sun never reaches. In these situations, shade is very often associated with dry soil. This is because tree branches or nearby structures deflect rainwater away, so less than normal falls on the soil. In addition, both trees and walls draw a great deal of moisture up from the soil. So the first rule when tackling a dry shady area is to add as much well-rotted organic matter as possible to improve the soil's water-holding capacity. If tree roots are close to the surface, do not try to dig in organic matter. Instead, use it the way it arrives naturally in woodland - spread a thick layer over the soil surface. Worms will gradually drag it down, and an annual top-up is all that is needed to keep a deep, moisture-retaining mulch in which suitable plants will thrive. Which are suitable? Well, if you plant 'normal' flowers in a dark situation, they simply grow tall thin stems that break easily, and unnaturally large foliage that is very prone to attack by pests and diseases. Worst of all, they will not flower. The answer is to plant dry shade-tolerant kinds. Some plants do, in fact, grow better in shade than anywhere else. Typically, shade-loving plants are not the most colorful ones, so it is no good expecting a riot of color. However, you can create a cool, sophisticated and charming display, which is much more suited to shady conditions.

Bergenia cordifolia

Flowers for dry shade

Alchemilla mollis
Arum italicum 'Pictum'
Bergenia
Brunnera macrophylla
Digitalis purpurea (foxglove)
Epimedium
Euphorbia robbiae
Hypericum 'Hidcote'
Iris foetidissima
Lamium (ornamental deadnettle)
Lunaria annua (honesty)
Liriope muscari
Pachysandra terminalis
Vinca (periwinkle)
Viola labradorica

Alchemilla mollis
(lady's mantle)

Even plants suited to growing in dry shade, such as the ones featured here, need to be kept watered in dry weather after planting. Continue to water them until they are well established.

Asperula odorata
(sweet woodruff)

Left: *Honesty flowers in its second year and then dies. Leave the plants to self-seed. Variegated forms, such as this Lunaria annua 'Alba Variegata', only develop variegation in the second year. Save the dried seedheads to use in winter flower arrangements.*

Right: Liriope muscari *(turf lily) is not very well known, but it is a useful and pretty, compact, clump-forming, low plant for dry shade. It flowers late in the season. Allow the clumps to spread; do not lift and divide them until it is absolutely necessary.*

Vinca major 'Variegata'
(periwinkle)

Geranium phaeum

Viola
labradorica
'Purpurea'

Right: Alchemilla
mollis *grows
almost anywhere
and self-seeds
where it is really happy.
The lime green flowers persist
for several months in summer,
and the pleated leaves are
attractive for most of the year.*

Flowers for sun and poor soil

On the face of it, a sunny site should be one of the easiest to choose plants for, and when the soil is deep, fertile and stays reasonably moist, the majority of annual bedding plants and herbaceous flowers will indeed do very well. But problems arise when the soil is thin, poor and dries out severely, and the site gets very hot. This commonly happens in front of a wall that faces the sun, although it can also be true of a small courtyard garden surrounded by walls that reflect the heat. Here, you must choose plants with great care. Unless you are prepared to improve the soil and water it regularly, avoid plants that simply need well-drained conditions; in most cases, they need soil that does not stay wet for long but does not dry out severely either. Opt for known heat- and drought-tolerant kinds and do not add a great deal of organic matter and fertilizer - these sorts of plants do not like it. They need hard conditions if they are to give of their best.

Generally speaking, perennial plants and bulbs are safest in this situation, as once they are established, they virtually look after themselves. However, if you grow heat-loving annuals (the ones with succulent leaves and whose flowers only open in sun), you will need to water them for some weeks after planting, as they will only tolerate the conditions when safely established. Drought-tolerant annuals are certainly the plants to choose for containers in this situation.

Right: Senecio 'Sunshine' (previously Senecio greyii) has tough, gray, felty leaves that prevent the plant losing too much water in dry conditions. Use it as an effective foliar foil to more colorful sunloving plants.

Cistus pulverulentus 'Sunset'

Dianthus (pinks)

Anacyclus depressus

Armeria maritima 'Alba'

Lavandula angustifolia
'Munstead'

Eryngium planum

Sempervivum
arachnoideum

Armeria maritima
'Rubra'

Plants for poor soil in a hot sunny spot

Acaena *(New Zealand burr)*
Armeria maritima *(thrift)*
Eremurus *(foxtail lily)*
Eryngium *(sea holly)*
Euphorbia cyparissias
E. polychroma, E. wulfenii
Gladiolus papilio
Helianthemum
Helichrysum amorghenum
H. angustifolium
Iris unguicularis
(winter-flowering iris)
Lampranthus *(use as annual)*
Leucanthemum hosmariense
Mesembryanthemum *(as annual)*
Nerine bowdenii
Portulaca *(as annual)*, Sedum
Sempervivum *(houseleek)*
Verbascum bombyciferum

Below: Allium sphaerocephalon *is a useful drought-tolerant summer-flowering bulb for planting in groups between shrubs. There is no need to lift the bulbs after they have flowered, as they are quite hardy.*

Flowers for rock gardens

Rock gardens are raised beds created deliberately to provide extremely well-drained conditions for plants from a mountainous native habitat. A thick layer of gravel and broken rocks on the surface of the bed allows fleshy plants to rest on a fast-drying surface to avoid rotting, and a high proportion of gravel in the soil beneath means that surface water runs away fast. However, a well-planned rock garden should not become bone dry in summer. The ideal rock garden soil is well drained but moisture retentive. This is easily achieved by mixing topsoil, gritty sand and gravel, and a low-nutrient form of organic matter (such as peat or coir) in roughly equal quantities. Rock plants are best planted in early spring, which gives them some time to establish before summer sun dries out the top of the bed too much. However, plants can be put in even when in flower, provided you water them for the first few months. Like other plants, rock plants vary in the amount of bright sun they like. Relatively few tolerate searing hot sun all day long - most prefer a few hours shade cast by nearby rocks or bigger plants. Choose a mixture of plant shapes and sizes for best effect, and aim for a long flowering season by selecting plants and bulbs that flower in succession from spring onwards.

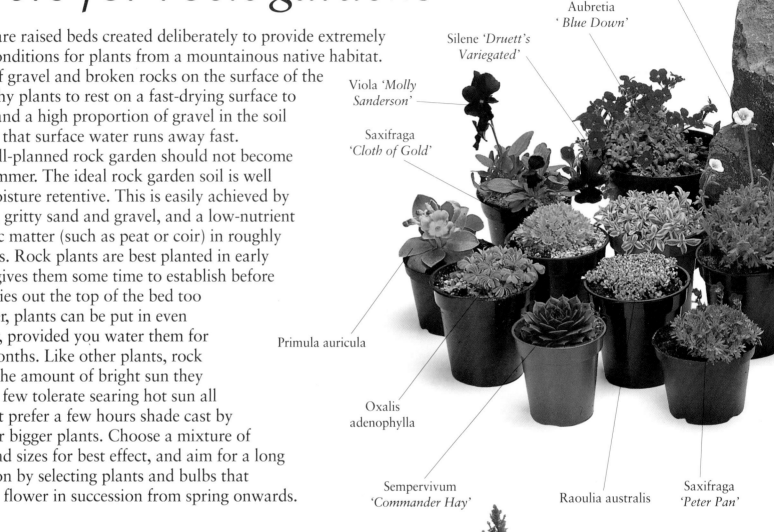

Saxifraga *'Fleece'*

Aubretia *'Blue Down'*

Silene *'Druett's Variegated'*

Viola *'Molly Sanderson'*

Saxifraga *'Cloth of Gold'*

Primula auricula

Oxalis adenophylla

Sempervivum *'Commander Hay'*

Raoulia australis

Saxifraga *'Peter Pan'*

1 *Spring is a good time to remedy any gaps in an existing rock garden. Before adding a new plant to the bed, carefully scrape away the topdressing of grit from the planting site using a narrow-bladed trowel.*

2 *Dig out a hole slightly larger than the pot in which the new plant is growing. Put the excess soil in a bucket so that it does not make the surrounding topdressing dirty.*

Arabis fernandii-coburgii *'Variegata'*

Aubretia *'Red Carpet'*

Aubretia *'Astola'*

Aubretia *'Blue Mist'*

Saxifraga *'Silver Cushion'*

Saxifraga *'Finding'*

Arenaria balearica

Saxifraga cotyledon *'Southside Seedling'*

Saxifraga aizoon *'Balcana'*

4 Replace the gritty topdressing around the new plant. This immediately makes it blend in with surrounding plants, and by working the grit well under the collar of the plant you help to prevent neck rot.

5 While obvious gaps need filling, leave an area of clear gravel round distinct groups of plants as this helps to show them off advantageously.

3 Knock the new plant carefully out of its pot and plant it into the prepared hole. To allow the new roots to grow into the ground, break up the soil at the base of the hole.

Planting through gravel

When there is not enough time to look after a conventional flower garden, a gravel garden may be just the answer. Here, appropriate flowers are grown through a deep layer of gravel, which acts as a permanent mulch, smothering weeds out and keeping moisture in. A gravel garden can be created from a tiny town courtyard garden or as a feature within a large area of paving or patio, but it is a good way to use a small front garden, particularly one that has to double up as car parking space occasionally.

To make a gravel garden, first strip the ground of turf - you can lay gravel around any large plants or shrubs you wish to keep. For a real no-labor garden, lay a sheet of slitted black plastic or special woven plastic landscape fabric over the area and then cover it with 2in(5cm) of gravel. This effectively prevents any weeds, and also stops flowers seeding themselves between the stones. Put in plants where required by brushing the gravel aside, cutting crosses in the plastic and planting through the holes. Otherwise, spread gravel straight over the leveled soil; a few weeds will get through, but flowers will be free to seed themselves. Simply weed out any that are not wanted. Choosing the right plants is a vital part of creating a gravel garden; aim for a Mediterranean look, full of spiky shapes and aromatic foliage plants, and decorate it with giant cobblestones and chunks of rock, alpine sink gardens and a range of terracotta pots to make the most of this unique ambience.

Plants for gravel gardens

Alchemilla mollis
Acanthus
Agapanthus
Artemisia
Artichoke
Bamboo
Crocosmia
Euphorbia wulfenii
Junipers
Hemerocallis
Kniphofia
Liatris
Ornamental sages
Phormium
Rosemary
Verbascum
Yucca

1 *Cover the soil with perforated black plastic or landscape fabric. If necessary, secure it with bent wire prongs pushed through into the soil to prevent billowing in a breeze.*

2 *Spread a 2in(5cm)-thick layer of gravel evenly over the plastic. Pea gravel with rounded edges looks best. If the gravel comes from the seabed, wash it first to remove the salt.*

3 *When you have decided where you wish to put in a plant, scrape back the gravel to reveal the plastic. Leave the spare gravel nearby as it will be replaced after planting.*

4 Make two cuts crossing each other in the middle of the planting site, each one about twice the diameter of the pot to allow room for working.

5 Peel back the corners of the plastic to expose the soil beneath; place stones or gravel on the flaps to hold them back while you plant.

6 Scoop out soil from the planting hole with a small trowel. If the soil was not first prepared for planting, dig a larger hole and add organic matter.

7 When the plant is out of its pot, make sure the planting hole is large enough for the rootball. Sit it in position, with its best side to the front.

8 Fill in the space around the rootball with soil and firm down lightly. Water well and then push back the plastic flaps, so that they fit snugly around the plant.

9 Holding the plant over to one side, sweep the spare gravel back round the plant with your hand, so that all the plastic is completely hidden.

10 Now the plant looks as if it has grown up naturally through the gravel. Plant large-growing subjects on their own; smaller kinds are best grouped together for greater effect.

Helianthemum 'Sunbeam'

Gravel garden borders

Above: Bergenia 'Beethoven'. Bergenia flowers, usually pink, mauve or red, appear in late winter and spring. The leaves are large and evergreen.

You can grow all kinds of plants in gravel: heat-loving, drought-tolerant flowers, such as red hot pokers, *Euphorbia wulfenii* and ornamental sages, are a popular choice, as they provide year-round effect. (They are also useful if the gravel area doubles as extra car parking space; plants of this size are easy to see and you can avoid driving over them.) However, many smaller flowers, such as spreading rock plants, hardy annuals and even wallflowers, are also happy growing in gravel. Where the gravel is placed over soil, they will often self-seed freely, creating attractive natural effects. Then, instead of just using gravel as a permanent mulch over flower beds, you could create a complete gravel garden, in which plants spread and self-seed, leaving meandering paths of clear gravel between groups. With a garden of this type, you often have to clear seedlings from pathways to make room to walk through once it is well established. This can make a very attractive, low-maintenance, natural or cottage-style garden, but do clear all perennial weeds out of the ground first. For a more formal garden, you could plant trailing annuals, such as nasturtiums or ornamental gourds, in beds on either side of a gravel walk and allow them to trail forwards over the path. This softens the hard edges of a gravel path under planted fruit tunnels or around the edge of a patio. Try a similar technique to make a slightly raised scree garden, using chunks of rock and gravel planted with choicer alpine flowers. In all but the smallest areas, sink stone slabs into the surface as 'stepping stones' to provide a firm surface for walking on or when weeding. The 2in(5cm)-deep mulch of gravel over already well-drained soil provides ideal growing conditions and allows plants to set seed to provide their own replacements.

1 Create a mini 'island bed' in a graveled area by grouping several warmth-loving and fairly drought-tolerant plants together. Make a separate planting hole for each one.

2 For the best effect, choose plants with different flower shapes and heights, and plant the tallest at the center and the shortest to the sides and front. Offer up the plants first to see how they will look.

Left: Being summer-dormant, spring bulbs team up well with other plants that tolerate hot, dry summers. Here, they combine with Euphorbia wulfenii, a singularly striking architectural plant for any gravel garden display.

4 This scheme would look equally at home in a cottage garden or a car parking area covered with gravel. In the latter case, roughly surround the plants with large stones as an early warning!

Above: Many rock plants are good subjects; these are Linum arboreum *and* Erinus alpinus. *The gravel mulch smothers out weeds and helps the soil to retain moisture.*

Osteospermum 'Stardust'

Armeria formosa

Stachys lanata

Lavandula 'Munstead Dwarf'

3 Continue adding plants, including some prostrate kinds that spill forwards over the gravel, so that it looks as if the plants had seeded themselves.

Helianthemum 'Sunbeam'

Nepeta mussinii

Flower carpets

Low, ground-hugging flowers look great planted as a carpet under trees and shrubs. To create the carpet effect, either use the same plant right across the border or mix different colors together (perhaps using several similar plants) for more of a 'Persian carpet' effect. A flowering carpet not only helps to set off the flowers above, but also creates a feeling of continuity, which visually pulls together a large border. It can also be a useful way of creating interest when the 'top tier' is out of season. For instance, under a predominately summer-flowering shrub border you could have a carpet of spring flowers, such as *Anemone blanda*, snowdrops or early-flowering dwarf narcissi (all of which tolerate light shade). Under a border that looks best in spring, choose flowers that look colorful all summer, such as *Impatiens,* which again tolerates light shade. If you want to use annual flowers such as *Alyssum* that need more sun, then keep the carpet towards the front of the border where there is more light. Sun-loving plants in deep shade will grow spindly and do not flower. Alternatively, use a carpet of one of the really ground-hugging hardy cranesbills to lend continuity right across the border. In the fall, a carpet of hardy cyclamen, fall crocus or colchicums looks utterly striking beneath a border filled with fall foliage colors.

Although flowering carpets are usually used to contrast with shrubs, there is no reason why you should not use the same idea in a border of tall, herbaceous flowers. Try low, shade-loving plants, such as hostas, *Lamium* (ornamental deadnettle) or *Pulmonaria,* for example. In an annual border, use a low carpet of *Impatiens* or try *Begonia semperflorens,* already in flower, to contrast with tall plants and striking shapes.

In light woodland or mixed borders Anemone blanda *makes a good substitute for the wild wood anemone. The corms have no right way up; to plant them, just drop them into small holes.*

Above: *A continuous cover of one kind of flower can also look very striking. Here,* Anemone blanda *has been naturalized around summer-flowering shrubs for spring color.*

Left: *A mixed carpet of spring-flowering bulbs for shady conditions, such as you find in light woodland or beneath shrubs in a border: dog's-tooth violet (Erythronium),* wood anemones *and* Anemone blanda.

Right: Cyclamen coum *thrives in short grass under trees and makes a splash of color in early spring. Large colonies gradually build up by self-seeding.*

Flowers for light woodland

Light dappled shade will support many flowers that dislike strong direct sun, particularly those that prefer moist soil. In light woodland, hardy cyclamen, trillium, dog's tooth violet and Solomon's seal thrive in diffuse light and a soil rich in leafmold. In a shrub border, herbaceous and other flowers, such as hellebores, lily of the valley, dicentra and hostas, will do well. Choose a mixture of low ground-hugging plants, those that are more upright or mound-shaped, and those that scramble up into the lowest branches, like some of the hardy cranesbills. These will all thrive on the same cultivation regime as the shrubs. Use a good general fertilizer in spring, as recommended, and mulch annually.

Right: Arum italicum *lies dormant in summer, but during winter and early spring the patterned leaves make a good foil for snowdrops and other early-flowering bulbs. Both enjoy moist shade.*

Below: Helleborus orientalis *makes a good spring-flowering clump in dappled shade in a border or light woodland setting.*

Carpet bedding

Carpet bedding was all the rage in Victorian gardens and today fashion-conscious gardeners everywhere are trying their hand at recreating antique flower beds. The essence of carpet bedding is to plant low-growing annuals close together to form patterns like a living Persian rug. You can use flowers or foliage or a mixture of both. The Victorians also created raised beds using wall-to-wall succulent plants. Many modern interpretations of the carpet bedding theme are in use around the world. One garden in Canada features life-size crinoline ladies, whose skirts are made from mounds of soil planted with *Impatiens*. They have wire torsos growing trailing ivy and are topped by genuine sun bonnets.

Choose plants that stay short and compact for carpet bedding schemes. One of the best compact foliage plants is *Alternanthera ficoidea amoena*, a half-hardy plant available in various foliage colors. Clip it regularly to keep plants tidy and to prevent them flowering. It is propagated from cuttings. You can achieve a similar effect using a dark-leaved lobelia, some kinds of *Amaranthus* or *Iresine* (bloodleaf). *Echeveria glauca*, a succulent plant with waxy blue leaves, is another popular foliage plant for carpet bedding. For flowering plants, choose almost any compact flowering annual: lobelia, alyssum, salvia, ageratum, etc. And as an authentic period piece, plunge a striking 'dot' plant - a symmetrically shaped plant, such as agave, yucca, cordyline or chusan palm - still in its pot, into the center of the bed. For a carpet bedding scheme to succeed, it is essential to plant in a soil that is totally free of perennial weeds. Deal with annual weeds immediately to avoid spoiling the pattern. Construct a 'bridge' over the bed - perhaps a plank raised up on bricks at each end - that allows you to weed without trampling over the plants.

Above: Formal beds outlined in dwarf box, with large patterns created in red and pink busy lizzie (Impatiens) and silver senecio (Senecio bicolor cineraria).

In cold climates, the succulents in this scheme are frost tender. Keep the plants in heated conditions from fall to late spring to avoid expensive losses.

Above: *An elaborate Victorian-style carpet bedding scheme needs a great deal of maintenance. A bed like this will have to be weeded every week.*

Left: *This formal Victorian-style carpet bedding scheme uses only foliage plants (*Echeveria glauca, Alternanthera *and* Sedum) *with a large variegated* Agave americana *as a dot plant in the center.*

Right: *This is a much more intricate Victorian-style pattern that combines* Echeveria glauca *with two kinds of* Amaranthus, *golden feverfew and flowering* Ageratum.

Ageratum

Golden feverfew

Amaranthus

Echeveria glauca

Right: *Here, feverfew and French marigolds are combined to make a delightful formal garden.*

Subtropical bedding

The Victorians often made subtropical borders with annual bedding plants set out in rows and tall, striking 'dot' plants, such as canna or standard fuchsia, standing over them in the center of the bed. Foliage plants, such as cordyline palm or castor-oil plant, were used as dot plants to contrast with the flowers beneath. Later on, plants were also used more informally, with large-leaved foliage plants grouped together with exotic flowers for a jungly impression. This type of display looks good on a patio using plants in pots. Plants with good flowers and large leaves, such as canna cultivars with bronze-purple leaves, are specially useful if you do not have room for many plants. In a garden with striking large-leaved evergreens, add pot-grown exotic flowers for a summer display. When planning a subtropical display, consider what to do with the plants in winter. Most subtropical-look flowers will need to be kept in a frost-free conservatory, sunroom or greenhouse. (Prune shrubby daturas and salvias hard so that they take up less room.) Alternatively, stick to annuals, cheap perennials that are easily replaced each spring, and tuberous plants, such as canna and ginger lily, plus other summer-flowering bulbs that die down in winter.

Suitable flowers

Anigozanthos *(kangaroo paw)*
Argyranthemum
Begonia grandis evansiana
(hardy in mild areas)
Canna, *Castor-oil plant*
Datura *(also called* Brugmansia)
Gazania
Hedychium *(ginger lily)*
Heliotrope
New Guinea hybrid Impatiens
Osteospermum *(hardy
in mild areas)*
Shrubby salvias, e.g.
Salvia fulgens, S. grahamii
(hardy in mild areas)

Below: *A subtropical corner, with canna and* Tithonia *(Mexican zinnia) adding to the 'hot' colors of dahlias, sunflowers and red hot pokers. Chusan palm and eucalyptus foliage in the background add to the effect.*

Cordyline australis
'Purpurea'

Coleus

Impatiens
(busy lizzie)

Impatiens
New Guinea Hybrid

Abutilon *hybrid. These
elegant plants are not
reliably hardy in cooler
climates during the winter.
Bring them into a frost-free
environment and cut them
back hard so that they take
up less room.*

Argyranthemum foeniculaceum
*(trained as a standard). This
plant is frost-tender; bring it
in or overwinter it as
rooted cuttings.*

Fatsia japonica.
*These plants will
survive outside
during the
winter, as long as
you plunge the
pots up to their
rims in the soil in
a sheltered spot.*

x *Fatshedera lizei
'Variegata'.
Overwinter this
plant as for Fatsia.*

Echeveria

Part Two

FLOWER ARRANGING FOR ALL OCCASIONS

Having seen how to grow a wide variety of flowers in the first part of this book, this section explores the fascinating and creative world of flower arranging. The opening pages explain the essential practical techniques that you will need to master and then, with this information literally at your fingertips, you are ready to tackle displays of your own.

Roses are an obvious choice, be they long- or short-stemmed, miniature or old-fashioned, and you will find plenty of ideas here for showing them off. Fuchsias and clematis might be considered less obvious candidates for indoor displays, but these popular garden flowers can make a considerable impact, either alone or combined with other subjects. The striking colors and unusual shapes of orchids make them ideal subjects for flower arranging and they are featured in a variety of displays. The lasting properties of orchids compares well with any other type of flower, even after being flown halfway around the world. In fact, even though most are nurtured in the carefully controlled conditions of a greenhouse, orchids will come to no harm in the home - provided they are carefully tended. The final part of this section offers a general overview of displays, from simple arrangements for everyday use to posies and garlands or a magnificent creation for that extra special occasion.

Left: Single blooms in individual containers make an impressive group. **Right:** *A lilac and apricot bouquet.*

Tools of the trade

Before you begin working with flowers there are a few practical points to be aware of. It helps if you know which are the right tools to choose and how to get the very best out of the materials that you will be using. One or two basic techniques, such as wiring dried flowers or rescuing blooms that look less than happy, are useful to know so that with a few simple skills at your fingertips you will be able to make any of the arrangements in this book. If you plan to work with dried flowers, you will need a few extra materials and equipment apart from good sharp florists' scissors or secateurs. Buy some small snips or even wire cutters and use these to cut stub, or rose, wire; do not be tempted to use your secateurs instead. You will need a reel of fine rose wire, as well as stiff stub wire, which is sold ready cut in a choice of lengths and usually by weight. There is a wide choice of special foam bases in many shapes for use with dried material, and apart from cones, rings and balls, you can always cut foam to any shape you choose for free-form decorations. A glue gun is useful for attaching dried whole seed pods or flower heads to a wreath or the edge of a basket.

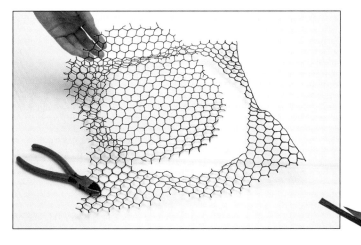

1 Crumpled chicken wire is strong enough to support roses in a shallow bowl. Cut out a rough circle with wire cutters, making the circle slightly larger than the area of the top of the bowl.

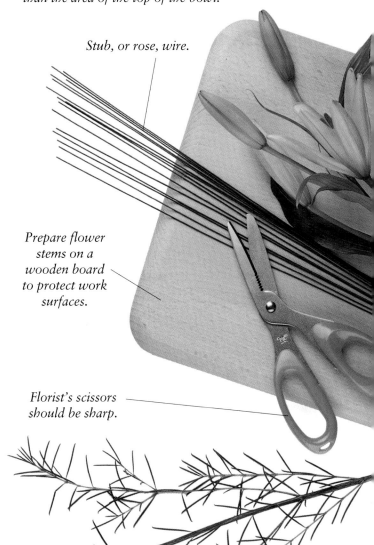

Stub, or rose, wire.

Prepare flower stems on a wooden board to protect work surfaces.

Florist's scissors should be sharp.

Left: *Glass beads are ideal for holding flower stems in position, particularly when just a few stems need supporting. They also look attractive in a modern, square glass container such as this and their soft green coloring creates a balance to the whole display.*

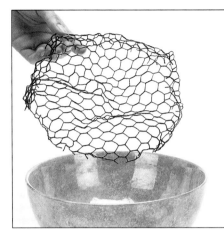

2 Squeeze the wire slightly so that it drops easily into the bowl and rests about halfway down. If it does not feel secure, attach it firmly to the inside of the bowl with some florist's tape.

Secateurs for cutting stems.

Use a hammer to crush woody stems.

Florist's tape.

Using floral foam

Floral foam is widely available from florists and garden centers. You will need different kinds for fresh or dried flowers, so make sure you choose the right one. Foam for fresh flowers must be thoroughly soaked before use and once the arrangement is finished, top up the water level regularly to keep the foam moist.

Right: One useful advantage of using floral foam is that you can cut it to fit any shape of vase. If the container is tall and narrow, use a sharp knife to cut a piece of foam to fit the neck, leaving a small amount protruding at the top to add height.

Left: Floral foam must be soaked before use to be really effective. Fill a sufficiently large bowl with water and keep the foam submerged until it sinks to the bottom. Then cut the foam to fit the shape of the vase.

Below: If necessary, you can secure floral foam to a dish with special florist's tape, designed to work with damp foam. One strip may be enough to do the job, but you can add as many pieces as you wish. Now you are ready to begin the display.

Preparing stems

Fresh flowers will repay a little time and effort spent on their preparation with a long and colorful life in an arrangement. If you buy flowers from a good market stall or flower shop, the chances are that they will have been conditioned. This means that stems will have been cleaned of foliage and recut, then stood in water for several hours to take up plenty of water. If you buy a bunch of flowers that have not been kept in water, the stems will have dried and possibly sealed over and you will need to cut them again and give them a drink. Give flowers picked from a garden the same preparatory treatment, preferably in the evening or early morning, which are the best times of day to gather material before too much moisture has transpired from the plant. Cut normal soft stems at a long slant to give the largest surface area possible to absorb water. A few very large flowers, such as delphiniums and amaryllis, have hollow stems that can be packed with a small plug of damp cotton wool to help them to drink.

Some flowers and foliage have stems that need to be seared or sealed to prevent them drooping or dropping petals. Hold each stem over a flame for a few seconds or stand it in a shallow depth of boiling water for two or three minutes. Poppies, euphorbia and some ferns all need this heat treatment. Boiling water can also revive wilting stems of flowers such as tulips, sunflowers, gerbera and mallow. Pour a small amount of water into a narrow-necked container and stand the flowers in this until they are revived. Remove any foliage that is not wanted on a stem or that will be below water. Submerged leaves rapidly cloud the water and make it smell and look unpleasant in a clear container.

Below: Clear unwanted foliage from the stems of chrysanthemums so that none of the leaves will be under water once the flowers are arranged. In water, leaves turn brown and rot away.

Wiring stems

The stems of some flowers, such as Helichrysum, *need to be wired before use. Remove the stem and push a stub wire down through the center of the bloom. Make a hook at the top and lodge this into the flower head. If possible, do this when the blooms are fresh, but they can be dry.*

Right: Always recut flower stems on a long slant so that they can take up as much water as possible. This simple arrangement begins with a few anemones laid around the edge of a shallow dish filled with water.

Anemones combine happily with all kinds of summer flowers to create informal, colorful arrangements.

Above: *Poppies need special treatment to last well in water. Stand the cut stems in a little boiling water for two minutes or seal them over a flame.*

Above: *Once you have cut and prepared the stems, stand roses in a deep container with a small amount of cool (but not icy) water and leave them to drink for several hours or overnight. This will prolong their life once they have been arranged.*

Woody stems

Many of the flowers and most of the foliage used in flower arranging comes from shrubby plants with strong stems that need slightly different treatment from soft-stemmed annual or herbaceous flowers. Flowers such as lilac are cut from large shrubs or small trees and their stems have bark over a solid woody stem. To prepare this sort of material correctly, cut the base of the stems on a slant and scrape or peel back the bark a little way to expose the stem beneath. Then either split the stem by cutting a few slices upwards with sharp secateurs or a gardening knife, or hammer the bottom few inches with a mallet. Remove unwanted leaves and small, twiggy branches that might get in the way of the rest of the arrangement or that would otherwise stand under water. Give all woody-stemmed material a good, long, conditioning drink in water at room temperature and leave in a cool place until you need to use it. Some foliage can be completely submerged in water, which makes it very crisp and unlikely to wilt later. Leaves such as beech, hornbeam and whitebeam, which you might use in a large-scale arrangement, benefit very much from this type of treatment. You will need a large container, and a bath is usually the best place to carry out this conditioning.

Above: It makes sense to remove sharp thorns from roses before arranging them. Use sharp scissors, secateurs or a special tool to clip them away. Some florists run up the stem with a blade, but this takes practice.

Rather than just slice across the stem, cut a slit a little way up the stem to reveal a larger surface area.

Above: Most roses have woody stems that need a little help to take in water efficiently from a vase or damp foam.

Left: *Always cut a rose stem at a sharp angle, leaving as large a surface area as possible touching the water. Ideally, you should recut the stem each time you take it out of water for a while, to expose fresh tissue again.*

Woody stemmed foliage requires the same preparation as roses.

Splitting or crushing stems may make them more difficult to arrange in floral foam.

Right: *Another method of increasing the surface area of the flower stem is to crush the lower part with a hammer or mallet. Make sure you do this on a wooden board or other solid surface.*

Basic floristry techniques

Once your flowers are conditioned and ready to use, there is little more to be done. For special posies, bouquets and circlets, it is useful to know how to wire flowers - here demonstrated with roses. This involves creating a thin and flexible replacement stem that you can move into any position. Also, a bunch of wire stems in a posy takes up less space than the same number of thick stems. Occasionally, a bunch of roses will wilt dramatically. The method described on these pages for saving them does not always work, but will usually bring them round. Wilting can be caused by stems drying out and then being unable to take up water properly, so always keep cut stems of unused roses under water, even while you are working and arranging. Finally, garden roses dry beautifully and very easily and it is well worth picking a few through the summer for this purpose. Dry them one at a time or several together and by the end of the summer you should have a beautiful collection for winter decorations.

Stopping the wilt

1 *Recut all the stems at an angle and stand them immediately in a small amount of boiling water for about 2 minutes.*

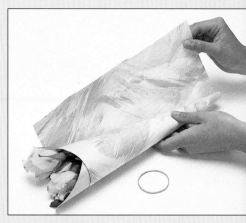

2 *Roll the bunch of roses tightly in some stiff paper and secure the wrapping with a rubber band. This also protects the roses during handling.*

Ready-cut stub wire for flower arranging is available in different lengths and thicknesses and usually sold by weight.

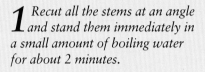

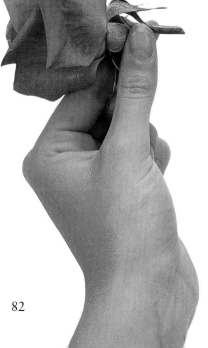

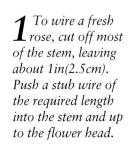

1 *To wire a fresh rose, cut off most of the stem, leaving about 1in(2.5cm). Push a stub wire of the required length into the stem and up to the flower head.*

Stem, or gutta, tape is available in green, brown and white. Green is the most useful for fresh bouquets and posies.

2 *Starting just under the rose head, take a piece of stem tape and twist and wrap it round the stem and down over the wire, too. It sticks to itself under pressure from your fingers.*

Home-dried roses

Drying roses at home is simple and made even simpler if you have a constant source of warmth over which you can hang the drying flowers. A solid fuel cooker or kitchen range is ideal, but a boiler, airing rack or even a greenhouse will do. The aim is to dry the flowers quickly to preserve their color. They shrink quite a lot, but also open out a little after they have been hanging up. Either hang up roses complete with stems (as shown here) or cut fresh rose heads, leaving a small piece of stem and attach a wire to them (see page 82). Hang them above the heat source, either singly or in a bunch. The wire will rust and bed tightly into the rose. As soon as the roses are thoroughly dried, remove them and store in a dry dark place.

3 Stand the flowers in their wrapping in a container of cool water for several hours or until the roses have revived and look fresh.

These roses have been left to dry on their own stems.

A fine bunch of fresh roses hanging up to dry.

The same roses, ready to use in an arrangement after drying.

Fairly full hybrid tea, floribunda or old-fashioned roses are the best for drying.

Scarlet red and yellow roses are two of the best colors for drying.

Using a classic porcelain vase

A classic flower-decorated porcelain vase needs a careful choice of flowers to fill it. Here, the painted flowers on the china provide the cue for what to put in it and the best colors to choose. Roses are the important feature, but they have been mixed with complementary garden flowers and foliage that form a framework and pleasing background to the blooms. This vase is designed to be seen from the front and therefore the arrangement faces forwards and is ideal to put on a side table, shelf or any piece of furniture that stands against a wall. The mix of colors may seem unconventional, but apart from one strong red accent, most are soft pastels. The final effect of the whole arrangement is harmonious and very pretty.

2 *Make an initial choice of flowers and bunch them to see how the colors work together. This will help you to estimate how much material you will need.*

Recut flower stems, then split any woody ones and trim away the lower foliage.

1 *Tape a block of damp floral foam securely into the vase leaving it well proud of the vase rim. Add more water as a reservoir to sustain the flowers once they have been inserted.*

In this arrangement, keep the amount of foliage to a minimum to leave space for plenty of different flower varieties.

Replace shorter-lived flowers as they fade to give the arrangement a longer life.

5 *Complete the arrangement with filler material, such as Alchemilla mollis and small-flowered, scented white 'Seagull' roses. Let a few flowers curve naturally down to the table.*

3 *Arrange tall stems in a fan shape across the back of the vase to create an outline and add a trailing stem at one side.*

The roses are old-fashioned and modern types. The multi-petaled old roses have the right feel for this traditional look.

4 *Continue filling in the display with shorter stems of phlox, alstroemeria and roses. Position them so that they are evenly spaced throughout and near to the front.*

Remember to top up the water level frequently, as there is a great deal of plant material in a small container.

85

1 *Begin by carefully cutting off any thorns and leaves that are likely to be under water in the vase. Leave any good foliage just below the flower head. Recut the base of the stem at a long slant.*

Pink roses in an elegant glass vase

Some vases are classic in their shape. This curvy glass one makes any flower displayed in it look elegant and timeless. However, the narrow neck means that only a few stems can fit in it, so choose roses with large flower heads for the maximum effect. A glass container will obviously show the stems inside, so be sure to strip off any small leaves and thorns leaving clean, neat stalks on view. Change the water daily too, so that it is kept clear and sparkling. Stand the finished arrangement in a light position and lower than standing eye-level, so that the perfect blooms are seen to best advantage. You could choose any color rose for this type of arrangement, from strong scarlet to soft peach, but it will have the most impact with just a single color. Here, the rose type is an exquisite pale pink hybrid tea.

3 *Start to arrange the rose stems one at a time in the vase, working round and spacing them evenly.*

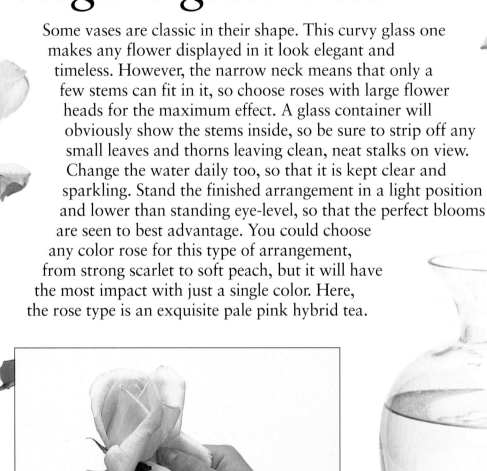

2 *Pull away any odd, stained, damaged or ugly outside petals to make a perfect bloom. Never take off more than one or two petals, otherwise the flower will look thin.*

86

Make the arrangement an all-round one to be viewed from any angle.

4 Add more blooms to create a cluster of flower heads in a curving shape that reflects the curves of the base below. Loosen the heads so that they are not crushed and have a little air and space around them.

If the stems are slightly short for the vase, fill the base with clear glass marbles.

Red roses, carnations and eucalyptus

1 Trim off lower stems and leaves from each spray of eucalyptus and cut all stems to the same length. Begin to put them into the vase, working round in a circle.

2 With the eucalyptus in place, add carnations throughout the foliage, working evenly all over the arrangement. Use some shorter stems at the outer edges.

3 Finally add the roses, spacing them out equally throughout the arrangement between the carnations. Aim to create a smooth continuous outline above the vase.

The blue-green eucalyptus leaves make a perfect foil for the strong crimson-red spray carnations and long-stemmed roses.

87

Bridesmaid's rose and ivy circlet

A small circlet of fresh flowers for a bridesmaid is not as difficult to make as it might appear. Once you have mastered how to wire each flower head and leaf, the rest is simple. Although the circlet will stay fresh for several hours, it is a good idea to make it as near to the event as possible. When complete, you can spray it with a fine mist of water to help it remain fresh, and then keep it covered under a single sheet of damp tissue paper until it is needed. The first thing to do is to measure the child's head accurately and to make the basic circlet, either with florist's wire or milliner's fabric-covered wire. Add a little extra to the circumference to allow for the thickness of the wires that attach the flowers to the circlet. Any small roses or rose buds are suitable, including miniature varieties.

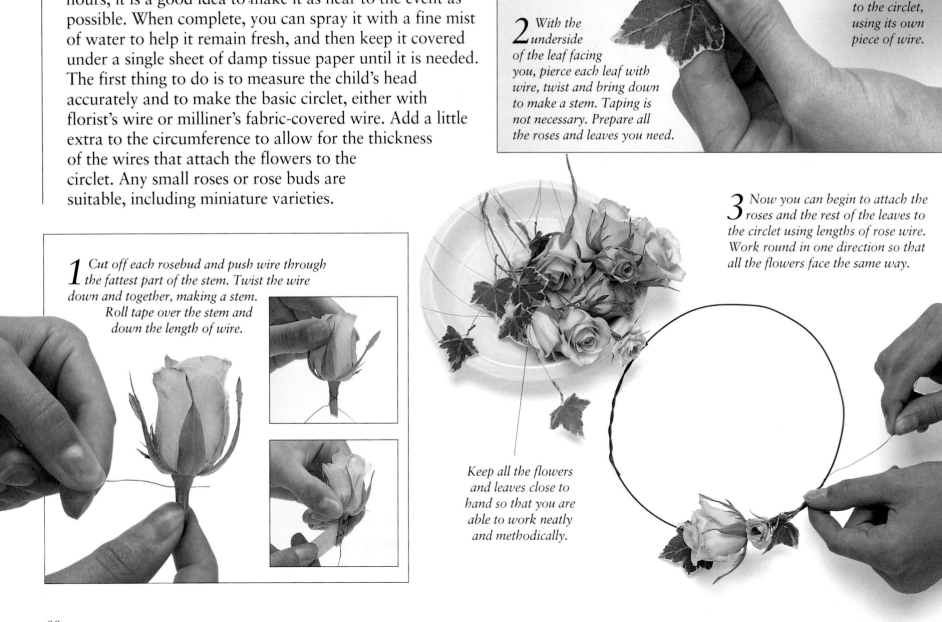

2 With the underside of the leaf facing you, pierce each leaf with wire, twist and bring down to make a stem. Taping is not necessary. Prepare all the roses and leaves you need.

Attach each leaf to the circlet, using its own piece of wire.

1 Cut off each rosebud and push wire through the fattest part of the stem. Twist the wire down and together, making a stem. Roll tape over the stem and down the length of wire.

3 Now you can begin to attach the roses and the rest of the leaves to the circlet using lengths of rose wire. Work round in one direction so that all the flowers face the same way.

Keep all the flowers and leaves close to hand so that you are able to work neatly and methodically.

If necessary, you can add more ivy leaves to fill in any large gaps or spaces in the final circlet.

A small-leaved variegated ivy makes the perfect foliage, as it is light and delicate but provides enough color contrast.

Ideal plants to use in a circlet

The fundamental construction of a circlet remains the same whatever plants you choose to use. For an older bridesmaid or a bride, you might want to use larger, more lavish roses to create a fuller and more stunning effect. Always choose foliage that is quite tough, such as ivy, leather fern, myrtle or something similar and that will not wilt too soon. Roses are always an excellent choice for a circlet, as they can be pinned through their calyx to keep them tightly in bud. Spray carnations, lily of the valley, stephanotis, ranunculus, lilies and orchids are just some of the other suitable flowers for this treatment. You could also consider many garden flowers, leaves and berries, which all make a lovely and informal addition to home-made bridal decorations.

4 Continue wiring the roses and ivy right around the circlet, alternating single larger roses with two or more miniature roses. Be sure to cover the circlet completely.

You could try adapting this scheme for making a circlet to decorate a hat. For added variety, choose larger and quite different roses.

Victorian rosebud posy in red, white and pink

Pure white spray carnations are a perfect posy flower. They last well and are solid and neatly shaped.

Small, hand-held posies, or tussie-mussies as they were once called, have been popular for centuries. Ideally, they should contain strongly scented flowers to give the most pleasure. This small posy is made in organized rings of different colors and types of flowers, based on the kind of posy a Victorian girl might have carried. A version of this idea is perfect for a small bridesmaid to carry at a wedding and there is no reason why a larger posy made with more rings of flowers should not make a beautiful bridal bouquet. The design looks complicated, but is very easy to make, as it falls naturally into place if the flowers in each ring are the same size. A rose or rosebud is the classic central flower, no matter what flowers make up the remainder of the posy. The last ring of a posy is often made from an edging of fern leaves or other foliage or even a paper frill to finish it off neatly. Here the fluffy flower heads of love-in-a-mist make an unusual and attractive edging.

1 Choose one beautiful rose bloom as the center starting point and hold it in one hand. Then begin to build up a ring of carnations around it, using the other hand.

Wiring at this point in the process means that you can relax and let go of the bunch if you need to.

You can use rubber bands, florist wire or string to tie the bunch of flowers together.

2 Complete the white circle and then start a circle of alternate pink roses and paler carnations outside it, holding it steady in one hand all the time. Tie it firmly after this stage.

Trim off the stems to the same length, using secateurs or a pair of sharp scissors.

Spray carnations or garden pinks have a sweet, spicy smell that blends well with the scent of roses.

4 The finished posy should be comfortable to hold, so do not be tempted to make it over large by bunching too many stems together.

3 Complete the posy with a final ring of love-in-a-mist or other appropriate flowers or foliage around the edge. Tie the whole bunch once again, winding wire tightly round the stems just below the flower heads.

Finish off the whole posy with a toning ribbon tied into a bow. This posy is decorated with wire-edged ribbon that is simple yet elegant.

Lapel decorations for that special occasion

There are still certain formal occasions when people are expected to wear a lapel decoration and other less formal events where it simply adds style and a touch of fun. There is no need to order an expensive one from the flower shop as it is a very simple piece of floristry to put together yourself, using home-grown flowers, as long as you chose varieties that will not wilt too quickly. A garden rose makes an imaginative and scented decoration compared with the dull and ubiquitous carnation. If you make it larger than a one- or two-flower version, you have a fine corsage suitable for a dressy suit, a ballgown or even a wedding hat.

3 *Take another flower, (here it is a freesia), and put it against the rose but extending slightly beyond it. Cut both the stems to the same length.*

Choose flowers that will stand this treatment, such as roses and freesias.

If you prefer, you could use different foliage, such as fern or a perfect rose leaf.

1 *Choose a perfect bloom that is just at the point of opening from the bud stage and cut it away from the main stem, trimming away foliage and thorns.*

2 *Select a short trail of variegated ivy and cut away the lower leaves, leaving the stem clear. The ivy should be slightly longer than the rose stem to show behind the bloom.*

1 *Choose a well-shaped, tightly closed bud and cut it off the main stem, leaving about 2in (5cm) of stem below the bud.*

4 Arrange the three stems of rose, freesia and ivy in your hand, with the rose at the front. If possible, hold the flowers against the clothes that are to be worn.

5 Bind the stems closely with green tape, working from the flower heads down the stems. Cover the cut stem ends and bring the tape back up, squeezing it tightly before cutting it.

Setting off with a fern

2 Snip off a piece of leather fern to put behind the bud. The fern should be a little longer than the bud.

3 Wrap tape tightly around both stems, twisting and squeezing as you work down. Wind the tape back up the stem a little way and then cut off.

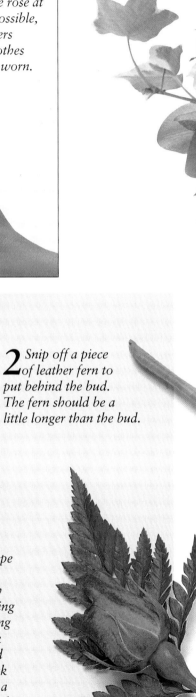

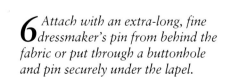

6 Attach with an extra-long, fine dressmaker's pin from behind the fabric or put through a buttonhole and pin securely under the lapel.

Pink Felicia roses in a moss-lined wire basket

Rose arrangements do not always have to be created on a grand scale or even be particularly large. Many varieties of garden rose lend themselves perfectly to simple, small decorations of the kind you might stand amongst a collection of favorite objects on a shelf or occasional table or in a guest bedroom. These simple, informal ideas are quick to produce and can make such a difference to any room. Both the ideas on these pages use scented roses and flowers, and both are displayed in unusual containers. Be open to new ideas when you come to select a vase and begin looking in the kitchen or china cupboard for old-fashioned bowls or molds or any suitable cookware that might make unusual flower containers. Small wire-mesh baskets are very popular for displaying all kinds of things and, when lined with moss, they are especially pretty for rose arrangements.

1 *Push a block of foam into the container and mark where to cut it. Leave it slightly proud of the rim to allow more height for arranging.*

1 *Soak some sphagnum moss until it is completely wet and then squeeze it until just damp. Line the basket on the base and all round the sides.*

Use suitable moss from the garden, or buy it from a florist or garden center.

The moss is just a disguise for the foam that goes inside the basket.

2 *Use a small cylinder of florist foam or cut a piece to fit snugly inside the basket. Make the foam wet and push it firmly into place inside the moss lining.*

You could line the base with plastic or stand the finished arrangement on a mat to protect the surface beneath.

Roses in a jelly mold

2 Remove the foam and slice it cleanly through with a sharp kitchen knife. Then wet the foam and push it tightly back into the container.

3 Begin to fill in the foam with stems of honeysuckle. Spread them all over the arrangement, spacing them out as equally as possible.

4 For extra variety, you can add a few different flowers, such as apricot digitalis and yellowy cream alstroemeria.

These are blooms from the delicately colored floribunda rose, 'Cafe'.

3 Fill the basket with small pieces of a floribunda or old-fashioned rose with buds and open flowers on the same stem.

4 Fill the basket generously so you have a full, rounded outline of roses. Mist it with a fine spray at regular intervals to keep both the moss and roses fresh.

The subtle pale pink hybrid musk rose 'Felicia' is generous with both blooms and scent.

Old-fashioned country roses in rustic baskets

Every kind of basket, whether it is smooth and shiny or rough and twiggy, has an affinity with roses. They complement each other very well and the rustic texture of willow, hazel or cane sets off the rich colors and velvety petals of garden roses to perfection. Old-fashioned, scented roses with wonderful, full-petaled heads in dense shades of raspberry, crimson and deep, glowing pinks are especially suitable for filling country-style baskets. The popular rambler 'Albertine', for example, with its lax stems and drooping heads, looks entirely at home in a twig basket. Both the versions of basket arrangements shown on these pages make use of roses in quantity alone, which produces a very strong look and undiluted texture and color. However, if you prefer, you could mix the roses with other flowers and plant material for a slightly different effect. If you do choose to do this, be sure to use at least a proportion of three-quarters roses to one-quarter other material.

1 *Metal foil is excellent for lining a deep basket as it easier to mold up the sides than plastic. It will provide a durable and waterproof 'container' within the basket. However, take care not to tear it as you put it in place.*

An 'Albertine' basket

Below: Plunge a complete block of floral foam under water and hold it there until it no longer bobs above the surface or as specified by the maker.

Left: Make the basket waterproof by lining with plastic sheet or foil. Working round methodically, fill the basket with roses, beginning at the base and leaving the top of the handle clear. Aim for a natural, tumbling effect as shown below.

The light crimson R. gallica 'Officinalis', also known as the Apothecary's rose, is the plain mutation of Rosa Mundi.

Try to mix lighter and darker shades of red and pink as much as possible for emphasis and contrast.

The pale mauve rose is 'Fantin-Latour', a beautiful, highly scented tall Centifolia rose.

This arrangement includes many old-fashioned types of rose, including the striped Rosa Mundi.

2 Drop a block of damp florist foam into the basket. A piece this size will not require taping, but you may need to wedge in smaller pieces of foam to fill in any gaps, depending on the size and shape of the basket.

3 Fill the basket with roses, starting at the front edge of one side and working across methodically. The roses at the back should be slightly taller than those at the front of the display.

Stand the basket on a mat in case moisture leaks onto polished furniture, and top up the foam with a regular spray of water.

4 The finished basket looks best when viewed from the front, so stand it at any height quite close to a wall or against a background feature.

Lilac and apricot bouquet

One of the most welcome gifts you can give to anyone is a bunch or posy of flowers, carefully put together and ready to stand in a vase or container of water. If the bouquet includes roses and flowers from your own garden, then the present is even more appreciated. Here, a subtle mixture of lilac, sweet peas and statice is combined with warm apricot roses to make a sweetly scented bunch. The easiest way to make a bouquet like this, whether it is big or small, is to make it in your hand, building it up flower by flower until it is complete and full. Then tie it and finish off with the flourish of a decorative bow in a matching color.

2 *First hold one or two stems tightly in one hand and add another flower with the other hand.*

At this stage, do not worry that the stems are all different lengths.

Sort out all the flowers you have so that you can see how they look together before bunching them.

1 *If the roses are floribunda types, begin by separating them into single stems and clean off the thorns and leaves.*

Dividing up a multi-stemmed rose will determine the length of the finished posy.

4 *When the bouquet is finished, cut the stems to make them all the same length and secure the whole thing with a rubber band or wire.*

5 *Lay the bunch of flowers down and wrap a ribbon around the stem, covering the rubber band. Knot the ribbon tightly and tie an attractive bow as a finishing touch.*

3 *Continue adding blooms, mixing the colors and varieties as much as possible and working round evenly. Hold the bunch as tightly as possible.*

Use good-quality ribbon to make the bouquet more of a special gift.

The recipient can remove the ribbon before standing the bouquet in water.

6 *The finished bouquet is pretty enough for a bridesmaid to carry. Try a pink and mauve version instead, or pale yellow mixed with pale blue, or simply white with green foliage.*

A beautiful blend of roses and peonies

There is a point in early summer when the old-fashioned shrub roses are in full bloom alongside the extravagant flowers of herbaceous peonies. As both species are multipetaled and are found in a similar range of colors, the two flowers look wonderful mixed together in relaxed arrangements. Although their origins are very different, they both have a very traditional, cottage garden look, best enhanced by simple china containers or old-fashioned pieces, such as this spongeware bowl. This is quite a small arrangement, but depending on how many blooms you are prepared to spare from the garden, you could make it any size you choose.

1 Crumple a square of wire netting so that it fits inside the bowl. You can tape it into place if you wish. Large-headed flowers with stems cut short are top-heavy and therefore need the support of wire in their container.

2 Cut each stem so that it is short enough to slot into the wire and yet leaves the flower head sitting just above the rim.

Use a peony, such as a double pink 'Sarah Bernhardt'.

Use small-scale wire netting from a hardware store or buy special plastic-covered wire from a florist.

3 *Begin by putting one flower at a time into the bowl, pushing the stem through the wire mesh. Work carefully round the bowl, keeping the blooms quite tight together.*

Mix the different shades of pink and red throughout the arrangement to achieve the maximum contrast.

4 *When you have used up all the blooms and the display is finished , give the flowers a light misting of water to keep them fresh.*

Peonies and roses will last about the same length of time as cut flowers.

Roses with a full cup shape and rich pink coloring, such as 'Constance Spry', are ideal for this display.

5 *The finished arrangement would look good below eye-level on a low occasional table, on a bedside table or as a dining table decoration.*

Old roses in blue-and-white china

Most of the old-fashioned and shrub roses produce one magnificent flush of flowers in midsummer, often a second flowering later on and occasional blooms throughout the season. When you cut blooms from them, it may seem as though you are wasting many buds that would have flowered later in the season, because the flowers are generally in clusters and their stems are short. However, they are such a pleasure to arrange, and fill the house with so much scent and color, that this is only a small sacrifice. Some varieties can be picked with very short stems for shallow bowls and similar containers. Support the stems with florist foam. The long, curving stems of many of the small-flowered species and hybrid climbing roses may not seem suitable for a vase, but many make lovely, if short-lived, displays.

1 Recut the stem at an angle and cut off and clear away any of the lower foliage and thorns that will be below the water level in the container.

2 Choose compatible containers in a range of shapes and sizes. Divide the roses into different types and put each type in a separate container.

A jug of climbing roses

Cut flowering stems off the very long trailing laterals of rambler roses, such as this 'Seagull'. Snip away faded flowers, the lower stems and foliage. A tall jug with a narrow neck keeps stems in place, but allows flowers to spread naturally.

Rosa gallica 'Officinalis' has light crimson petals, golden stamens and typical tough gallica foliage.

4 Position the three small arrangements, with the tallest at the back. Leave enough space around them so that each is clear to see, but together they make a harmonious single group.

Old garden roses

Red/purple
Tuscany Superb
Charles de Mills
Baron Girod de L'Ain
Reine de Violettes
Mme. Isaac Perreire

Pink
Comte de Chambord
Petite de Hollande
Celestial
Fantin-Latour
Queen of Denmark
Louise Odier
Reine Victoria

White
Boule de Neige
Comtesse de Murinais
Shailer's White Moss
Blanchefleur
Mme. Hardy

3 Place the second variety in a different container. Keep the roses with the longest stems for the tallest jug or vase.

The pretty buds and strong green foliage of this 'Président de Sèze' add extra interest.

'Ferdinand Pichard', a fine striped rose, has neat, organized flowers and is repeat flowering.

Use crumpled wire or florist foam if the roses are difficult to arrange in a bowl of this shape.

Yellow roses in a pink glazed bowl

Traditionally, the classic rose bowl for displaying perfect roses is round and quite shallow, with a gently curving outline. However, it is not always easy to support roses with heavy heads in a bowl of this shape, and you will have to find a method of holding each stem in place away from its immediate neighbor. Some rose bowls have an integral wire mesh disc on top of the rim, but a simpler and cheaper solution is to use any favorite bowl of the right shape and to add your own crumpled chicken wire or plastic-coated wire netting. Mix in another type of flower or foliage to conceal the wire mesh below and to provide a contrasting background to set off the color and shape of the blooms. Here, bright acid green *Alchemilla mollis* complements rich yellow 'Graham Thomas' roses.

1 Begin by cutting out a rough circle of small- to medium-sized wire netting with wire cutters. Make the circle slightly larger than the area of the top of the bowl.

2 Squeeze the wire a little so that it drops easily into the bowl and rests about halfway down. If it does not feel secure, attach it firmly to the inside of the bowl with florist's tape.

Plastic-coated wire lasts well and does not damage precious china, glass or metal containers.

3 *Add sprays of Alchemilla to the bowl, covering the wire completely and creating a soft, curving outline. The Alchemilla can extend beyond the edge of the bowl to make a wide, low display.*

4 *Space the roses evenly throughout the arrangement, inbetween the foliage. Leave the center stems a little longer than those around the lower edge. Give a fine mist of water.*

'Graham Thomas' is a good choice of rose as a cut flower, as it keeps its color well and has pretty cup-shaped blooms.

5 *This arrangement would look good as the centerpiece of a large dining table or on a low table where it can be viewed from above.*

The pink, sponged glaze on this 1950s bowl is an effective foil to the green and yellow flowers.

105

A traditional wreath of striped roses

Garlands or wreaths are a good way of making the most of a few special flowers. They have lost their old image of only being hung on a door at Christmas and are used decoratively throughout the year for any special occasion or they can be laid flat as a table centerpiece. The traditional method of making them used a wire and damp moss base with the flowers wired on, but these days the easiest way is to use a ready-made foam ring. Roses are ideal as flowers to use in wreaths and garlands along with some other foliage or plant material to work as a filler. You could, of course, make a very beautiful and luxurious wreath with just roses, but a filler of some kind is useful for covering the foam completely and adding contrast to the flowers. A wreath made in this way on a damp foam base will last for several days, especially if you keep it moist with an occasional fine spray of water.

You will need a loop of wire if you intend to hang the wreath vertically.

Follow the maker's instructions on soaking the foam so that it is neither too wet nor too dry.

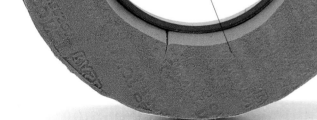

2 *Using short stems of gypsophila as a filler, work around the ring, covering it completely.*

3 *Next, begin to add short stems of dianthus, spacing them evenly throughout the gypsophila.*

4 *Add the roses, filling the spaces between the dianthus to create a densely textured effect.*

1 *Make a small loop around the ring with some garden wire. Then soak the ring in water before filling it with flowers. Work with the ring held vertically or horizontally, whichever is comfortable for you.*

Candlesticks adorned with miniature roses

Roses always look good used as table decorations, and partnered with candlelight they look even better. Here, two very ordinary recycled glass candlesticks have been given a glamorous treatment with a clever ring of foam around them to hold small red roses and sprigs of fern leaf. The idea can be adapted for any type of candlestick as the candles in effect hold everything in place. Just be sure to make the foam ring big enough to hold the stems securely and do not let the candles burn right down too near to the flowers. Any small-flowered rose or miniature rose will be suitable for this arrangement and ivy leaves could replace the fern if you prefer. Colorful candles look good as a contrast to the flowers, or choose plain cream or white ones for a more classic look.

1 Cut small pieces of foam about 1in(2.5cm) thick. Then make a hole right through the foam by pushing down with the candle.

2 Mark out a circle around the hole, about 3.5in(9cm) across, depending on size of candles and holder. Cut it out with a sharp knife and soak the foam.

3 Prepare the roses and foliage by separating the flowers from the bunches and cutting the stems short. Do the same with the foliage.

You can pull apart a stem of leather fern into several small leaves.

4 Place the foam ring on the candlestick and push the candle through. Use small pieces of florist fixing tape to secure it if necessary.

Put the foliage in place as a filler and to provide a contrast to the flowers.

Most candlesticks have a suitable 'drip tray' on which you can support the foam ring.

This small red rose looks pretty in bud and when it has opened out. Use of a mixture of buds and open flowers in the arrangement for maximum interest.

5 Once you have a basis of green foliage all over the foam, begin to add the roses and buds, working methodically around the ring.

6 The finished decoration could be a matching pair of candlesticks or a single decoration. One for each guest would look pretty on a table setting.

Roses, scabious and cornflower table decoration

1 *Cut a piece of foam to the right thickness for the dish then mark out a circle by pressing a round object onto the foam. Cut the foam to shape using a sharp kitchen knife.*

Some people simply cannot bring themselves to cut a rose with a very short stem. However, once you have come to terms with the idea, you can begin to make all kinds of unexpected and unusual decorations and arrangements in a variety of containers. The flower heads become a means of creating color and texture to make things such as table decorations. You will need a suitable container and this can either be part of the overall arrangement or simply a tray or base that is hidden by the display but holds the water and florist foam. In the example shown here, a blue-and-white china soup plate makes the perfect container, providing an area deep enough to hold the foam, but pretty enough to make an edging to the finished display, which in turn becomes part of the table decoration.

3 *Position the damp foam in the center of the plate and cut all the flowers short, so that the stems are only about 2in(5cm) long. Put the first rose in place in the center.*

Arrange a ring of cornflowers right around the central rose.

2 *Wet the foam as usual and push it onto a pin holder, as here, or use a special foam holder. An old-fashioned pin holder is good and heavy. A foam holder will need to be taped in place.*

4 *Make a ring of scabious flowers outside the cornflowers, pushing the stems into the foam to secure them. The delicate mauve of these blooms tones pleasingly with the bright blue of the cornflowers.*

Arrange the flowers as close as possible to each other without squashing them.

Variations on a theme

In the arrangement featured here, the central rose is a deep pink 'Madame Isaac Perreire' and the paler roses around the edge are 'Celestial', a beautiful alba rose. You could completely change the look of this display by choosing different colors. Try a deep yellow central rose with the same mauve and blue flowers in between and a paler creamy yellow rose around the edge. Or you could try a very deep purplish-red central rose, again surrounded by rings of mauve and blue flowers, and alternate crimson and pink roses for the outside ring. Alternatively, you could achieve a totally different look with all white roses and soft greeny gray foliage or flowers between the two rings

5 *Finish with a final ring, this time of roses, which simply sit inside the rim of the dish. Top up the dish with water for the roses and to keep the foam damp.*

Tea cups and a rosy hat

A very simple but effective way of using garden roses is to line up a row of three, four or five cups and saucers and use them as small vases to hold single blooms or little bunches of your favorite roses. You could choose cups all in shades of pink or with a rose-decorated theme, or you might prefer plain white cups or pale green ones, which would look equally pretty. The finished group can stand in a line along a shelf or on a windowsill or down the center of a table. On a small round table they might look better grouped closer together. Here we also look at how to decorate a summer hat with a few special roses for a grand occasion.

1 *Choose an attractive group of cups and saucers and fill them with water. Select appropriate roses for each cup.*

Cut stems to the right length and remove any unwanted foliage.

Split the stems from the base upwards to help the roses take up water.

2 *Make small arrangements in each cup, adding a few pieces of foliage to one or two if you wish. You can mix different varieties or keep to a single type.*

A hatful of roses

This is 'Aloha', a climbing rose with an old-fashioned look and beautiful rich color.

1 *Choose two perfect matching blooms and trim, leaving about 3in(7.5cm) of stem and leaf. Wrap tape around the stem, making sure that you enclose the cut end.*

3 *Arrange the cups, balancing light and dark flowers throughout the line and mixing solid color cups with lighter, floral sprigged ones.*

Reine des Violettes

3 Using fine rose wire, attach the rose stems to the hat by threading the wire right through the straw inside the crown and out again. Twist the wire tightly round the stems a few times and neatly cut off any extra wire.

4 Fold a chiffon scarf around the base of the crown or wrap a wide ribbon round it to cover the rose stems. Knot or tie into a bow at the back of the hat.

2 Put the two roses together, one just above the other and bind them together with tape to make one stem. Position the roses on the hat at the base of the crown at one side.

'Celestial' has very pretty grayish green foliage that sets off its pale pink flowers very well.

Rose 'Félicité Parmentier'

Rose 'Fantin-Latour'

Rose 'Président de Sèze'

The deep, glowing purple-red of the gallica rose 'Charles de Mills' matches this charming Victorian tea cup.

Roses in clear glass

Sometimes you need to make a table decoration or arrangement for a room quickly and nothing could be faster to put together than these two ideas. Both rely on sparkling clean and shiny glass, so the first thing to do is to spend a couple of minutes buffing the glass until it glitters. Pour the water in carefully, in order not to splash the sides and create tide marks and spots on the glass. Economical with flowers as well as time, these ideas are the perfect way to achieve real impact with very little effort. For a different effect, float single flowers on small individual glass dishes or glasses for a very pretty table setting for a special meal.

Choose a rose variety that has plenty of interest inside the flower, either with lots of petals like this one or with a pretty center and stamens.

Cut the stem away from the rose head at the point where the stem fattens out into the flower.

1 *Decide how many blooms you have room for in your container and prepare each rose the same way. A good solid rose such as 'Graham Thomas' is best for this treatment.*

2 *The water should be just deep enough to allow the flowers to float easily. Lay the bloom very gently on the surface, so that the flower head does not become too waterlogged.*

On a hot night, you could add a few ice cubes to the water or perhaps a few drops of rose essential oil for added fragrance.

Adjust the level of the water according to the height of the bowl and the angle from which it will be seen.

'Graham Thomas' is one of the new breed of English roses, old-fashioned in style, but repeat-flowering.

3 Continue adding blooms. The final number will depend on the size of the bowl, but there should be enough room so that they do not all crowd each other but can float freely.

Bottled roses

1 Choose two bottles that relate in shape but vary in height. Fill with water. Leave a long stem on one rose but trim away lower leaves.

2 Stand the first rose in a tall bottle and then put the second rose in the smaller bottle. Adjust the height of the roses if necessary.

3 Stand the bottles in their final position, one in front of the other. Turn the roses so that they face forwards but do not cross each other.

1 *Before mixing the gel with water, read the manufacturer's instructions carefully and check the proportion of gel to water. Put a spoonful of gel into a large bowl.*

Fuchsia heads in a blue glass bowl with gel

Displaying fuchsias as individual blooms gives you the opportunity to discover the beauty and complexity of each flower. You can show off your favorite varieties and pick the most colorful combinations to make a spectacular table centerpiece. When a bloom is upturned, it is possible to see clearly how each flower is constructed and just how pretty the color combinations of petals are; it is as if you had a completely new species of flower to use. If you cut off the stem just below the lower petals, each bloom will last very well as a cut flower, even without any stalk. Arranging and displaying the fuchsias in a flower gel gives them stability and the best conditions for lasting. The gel is sold in the form of dry crystals and swells dramatically when water is added. It makes a superb medium for this kind of arrangement, holding the bloom in place and providing water to the cut stem. You can even add food coloring to it to create different and exotic effects without harming the flowers.

2 *Add the required quantity of clean, cold water and stir well for a few seconds. Now leave the gel to absorb the water to its maximum capacity.*

3 *The gel will be ready to use after about ten minutes. Tip most of it into a large shallow bowl and the rest into each small glass.*

4 *Prepare some single blooms from the stems of fuchsias. Cut each flower off just where the stem finishes under the head. Choose perfect specimens that are just fully opened.*

5 Place the fuchsia flowers into the bowl, arranging them into the gel which will support them in an upright position. Leave space around each bloom. These are Reading Show.

Mixing several varieties together makes the most impact in such a simple arrangement.

Seeing the fuchsias in profile sheds a whole new light on them as flowers.

Marinka

Rufus

Ben's Ruby

Billy Green

6 Arrange the two small glasses in the same way. The finished bowl looks superb, especially as the strong color of the glass contrasts with the rich reds and purples of the fuchsias.

Mixed fuchsias in a moss-lined basket

This is a lovely way to display different fuchsia varieties together in a fresh and informal arrangement. The green wire basket and moss look just right with the arching sprays of fuchsia. The fuchsias used here are all quite similar types, with medium to small flowers, both single and double. Basket types are suitable, as well as upright-growing kinds. Cut them from large plants and leave the foliage intact to provide color contrast and definition. It would be an ideal way to display branches of hardy types that you have picked from the garden and brought indoors. Treat the stems of fuchsias as you would any other cut flower material. Split woody stems a little to allow better absorption of water and cut green stems at an angle neatly and cleanly. You could adapt this idea and create it using a basket made from other material, although the moss is an important part of the design and should be clearly visible through the sides of the container.

5 Start to push the fuchsia stems into the foam. The aim is to create a pleasing all-round arrangement that mixes the varieties fairly randomly.

1 Start by lining the wire basket with fresh, damp moss. You will find it easier to work using several small pieces rather than struggling with one unwieldy mass.

2 Push the pieces of moss against the sides of the basket and as far up as possible while the basket remains empty.

3 Now line the basket with a piece of thin black plastic cut roughly to shape. This will hold in the moisture later on.

4 Cut a block of damp flower foam to fit inside the basket, stopping just below the top of the basket. Put it into position.

118

6 *Continue building up the arrangement, adding more stems to make a fairly dense mixture. Let one or two stems drop down low at the front and sides of the basket.*

Snowcap

Pacquesa

Dollar Princess

Margaret Brown

Rufus

Mary

7 *Stand the finished basket either at table height or a little higher to appreciate the hanging fuchsia flowers better. Spray occasionally with a fine mist of water to keep the basket fresh.*

Fuchsias, pinks and lilies in three-tiered glass

This is a classic and very glamorous arrangement for a special occasion. Although it looks grand and formal, it is exceptionally easy to put together. You will need two cake stands that balance on one another and both should be just deep enough to hold a little water for the flower stems. The lilies and pinks create a good foil for the more delicately shaped fuchsia flowers that tumble downwards from the display. The whole idea is reminiscent of designs used in Victorian times to decorate buffets and dinner tables, as fuchsias were very popular during that period. If possible, construct the arrangement in situ, as it is very difficult to move once it is made up. You could try a different version of this idea using a thin layer of damp moss on each stand and setting the flowers amongst it. This would work well if the stands were made of china rather than glass or where they are too shallow to hold enough water.

3 Take a stem of lilies with two or three blooms and cut the stem short. Lay it under water at one side of the lower stand.

1 Choose two suitable glass cake stands and a single goblet-shaped glass for the top layer. Make sure that the top stand sits steadily on the one below.

2 Gently pour a little water from a jug so that it just covers the lower stand. Then do the same to the second one and fill the goblet.

4 Add a sprig of fuchsia alongside the lilies and put three pinks and a sprig of fuchsia on the opposite side of the upper stand.

5 Finally put several stems of fuchsias into the top glass filling it all the way round. Choose a small-flowered, dainty variety.

6 Keep the water level topped up in the stands, so that the flower stems are always under water. You will find that water evaporates quickly from the large area, so keep an eye on it.

Beacon Rosa

Beverley

Rufus

Beads, floating candles and fuchsia heads

Using fuchsia flowers upturned gives them an exotic look and by massing together several different varieties you can transform them into a stunning display. Fuchsia heads happily float in shallow water and if you combine them with glittering glass beads and flower candles in a round glass bowl, they make a party decoration for a sumptuous summer evening. Strong-colored varieties were deliberately chosen for the arrangement featured here to create the most impact, and the mixture of narrow-petalled types with rounder shapes gives a lovely lattice effect. Similarly, the decision to choose some very small flowers and mix them with large ones adds greater interest and impact than using blooms all of the same size. The candles are in two shades of pale pink and the beads are in a range of soft pearlized pinks. For a variation on this theme, you could combine some fuchsia flowers with loose petals from roses, or float other flowers and foliage among the fuchsias. It is always pleasing to include some flowers or foliage that have a fragrance to an arrangement like this.

2 *Next, place four or five small floating candles into the water. Be careful not to get water on the surface of the candles if you wish to light them later on.*

3 *Prepare a selection of fuchsia flowerheads by cutting the stems just below the point where they end in a small green lump.*

Cut the blooms neatly from their stems, using sharp scissors.

4 *Once you have cut all the flower heads, begin to float them on the water. Arrange all the different types at random, but try to mix the various kinds as thoroughly as possible.*

6 *This display combines deep maroon and purple fuchsias with shocking pinks and reds. Salmon pinks and orange shades would make a different, but equally effective design.*

Bob's Best

Delta's Wonder

Dollar Princess

If you light the candles, do not leave them unattended.

5 *Place the finished display on a low surface or in the center of a dining table for maximum impact. Ideally, the arrangement should be viewed from above.*

Peter Bielby

Baroness Van Dedem

The large furled petals of Cecille are shown off to great effect when upturned in this way.

Pink fuchsia candlesticks to adorn your table

Any arrangement or idea that exploits the fact that fuchsias hang their blooms downwards is bound to be successful. This idea uses just a few pieces of fuchsia or two different varieties but both basically pink. The leaves are also used as part of the whole arrangement and to help hide the foam ring, which is the crucial part of the idea. The candles can be lit or not, depending on how you wish to use the finished candlesticks. If you do light them, always stay in the room in case they burn down too far. Fuchsias are surprisingly good-tempered as cut flowers and should last well in a decoration such as this. After a day or so, check whether the foam is drying out and if it is, spray the ring with a fine mist or direct a little water straight onto the foam with a narrow spout. These white china candlesticks are particularly effective but you could use any design or color, or even plain, clear glass. Choose a medium-sized fuchsia flower that is quite light and dainty for a display such as this and avoid the very large, multipetaled types that would look wrong and top heavy.

1 Use a metal cookie cutter to cut rings from a piece of well-soaked flower foam about 0.8in(2cm) thick.

2 The candle makes the perfect cutter for the inner hole. Just push it down and through the foam. The candlesticks must have a large enough rim for the foam to sit on.

3 Put the candles firmly into place in the candlesticks and slide the rings over to sit on the tops of the candlesticks. They should be secure enough not to need tape.

4 Snip off small sprigs of fuchsia from larger stems. To achieve this effect, you will need one or two flowers, a few buds and perhaps some leaves on each little sprig.

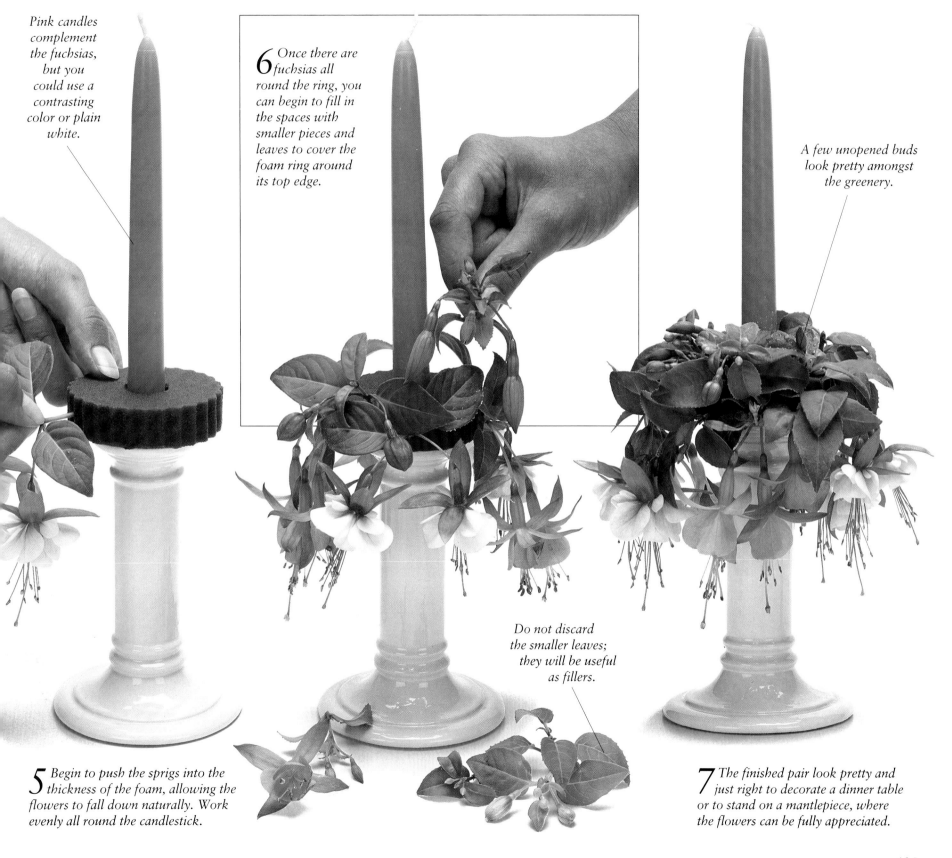

Pink candles complement the fuchsias, but you could use a contrasting color or plain white.

6 *Once there are fuchsias all round the ring, you can begin to fill in the spaces with smaller pieces and leaves to cover the foam ring around its top edge.*

A few unopened buds look pretty amongst the greenery.

Do not discard the smaller leaves; they will be useful as fillers.

5 *Begin to push the sprigs into the thickness of the foam, allowing the flowers to fall down naturally. Work evenly all round the candlestick.*

7 *The finished pair look pretty and just right to decorate a dinner table or to stand on a mantlepiece, where the flowers can be fully appreciated.*

A bouquet of tumbling dendrobiums

You will need to master the basic skills of wiring and mounting flowers before tackling a project such as this, but the reward for a little extra care is a bouquet full of life and movement, created as much by the space around the flowers as by the component parts of the design itself. When viewing the bouquet from behind, the wires should resemble the spokes of a wheel, each one radiating neatly from the central securing point. Since these wires form the handle of the bouquet, reduce them to a length that allows the bouquet to balance easily in the hand without tilting forward. Tape the wires together with stem tape and finally, for appearance and handling comfort, bind the bouquet neatly and securely with a narrow satin ribbon.

Condition the foliage and flowers for several hours in water before starting to make the bouquet.

4 *Mount individual leaves using a silver wire. Stitch from the reverse, then wind the silver wire around the leaf stalk and finish by covering with tape.*

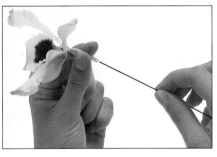

1 *Insert a wire through the stem into the back of the flower. The wire must be strong and springy, allowing the flower to 'bounce' without bending.*

2 *Pass a silver wire through the back of the flower, then wind it around the stem to hold it firmly in place. You will need a steady hand!*

To mount the flowers, use a very fine wire. Heavier flowers may require a thicker gauge wire.

3 *Cover the flower stalk and wire with a thin twist of stem tape, starting from the back of the flower head.*

5 *Secure and tape single flowers with the ivy leaves to form individual units. Take five units and arrange them into the basic design. Fix in position using silver wire to form a central securing point at the back of the bouquet.*

Soft green ferns contrast with the dark green of the ivy leaves.

You can substitute the individual flowers of Dendrobium Montrose AM/RHS used here with a range of other orchids in exciting shapes and colors.

Nephrolepis *fern*

Hosta undulata

The dark ivy leaves accentuate the central focal point of the design.

6 *Taking the wires through the securing point, add two central flowers, placing them close together to form the focal point.*

7 *With all the flowers in position, add weight to the center of the design using ivy and hosta leaves. Then incorporate Nephrolepis* fern *to further accentuate the focal point.*

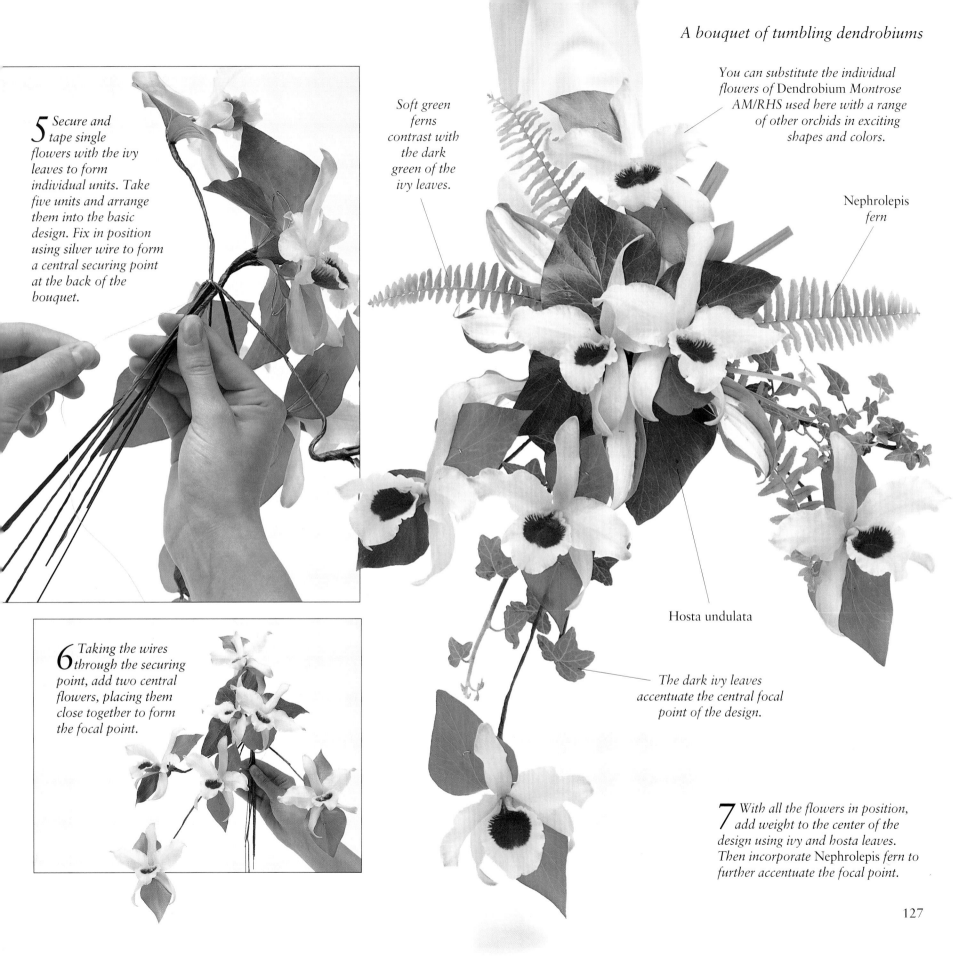

127

A crescent-shaped handspray

Using a foam bouquet holder to create this striking crescent-shaped handspray allows you to feature flowers and foliage on their own stems. This not only looks more natural, but means that once inserted into the wet foam, they last a long time. Naturally, the character of the design will depend on the type and color of the orchids you feature. Here, the choice of *Cochlioda noezliana*, with so many flowers elegantly displayed along their wiry stems, lends great movement to the design. The single flowers of *Epidendrum radicans* have been mounted on long thin wires to soften the whole appearance, while the more solid shape and severe lines of *Bifrenaria harrisoniae* form the focal point. These flowers also have the added bonus of being heavily scented. Do not be tempted to overcrowd the handspray with an excess of flowers; the impact of the design relies on the ability to see the form of the individual flowers. As you build up the design, be sure to take advantage of any natural curves, either on the stems of the orchids or the foliage, that will help to create and maintain the crescent shape. This colorful handspray would be perfectly suited as a presentation bouquet.

1 Wet the foam bouquet holder, but do not oversoak it. Insert sprigs of foliage to outline the shape of the bouquet before adding any flowers. Allow the natural movement of the foliage to give a free-flowing look.

Remove the leaves and side branches from the stems before inserting them into the foam.

Cymbidium corsage

Cymbidiums are ideally suited to create this double corsage. Wire and tape the flowers and foliage, using the thinnest wire that will support each component part. Choose foliage to complement the colors of the orchids used.

Above: *Arrange the foliage around the flowers, uniting the wires to form a 'stem'.*

Right: *Cut to the required length and tape everything firmly.*

The soft green foliage of juniper provides an excellent foundation for the handspray.

2 *Push the flower stems deeply into the wet foam of the holder so that they are held firmly. Add more foliage and continue to build the bouquet into the crescent-shaped design.*

The rich dark foliage gives depth and forms an integral part of the design.

3 *Develop a focal point by using more dominant flowers in the center. All the flowers and foliage must appear to spring from one point deep within the bouquet.*

The fiery orange-red flowers of Cochlioda noezliana.

The large fragrant flowers of Bifrenaria harrisoniae form the focal point of the bouquet.

Individually wired flowers of Epidendrum radicans provide a delicate, softening effect.

129

A hand-tied bouquet

This hand-tied bouquet is a simple gathering of flowers and foliage assembled in the hand. When choosing flowers and foliage to create a hand-tied bouquet, select stems of a good length, so that when the bouquet is complete you can cut the ends off level, and when placed in a vase, they will all be below the water level. First remove all flowers and leaves from the bottoms of the stems that would otherwise become damaged during the construction or tying. Condition both the flowers and foliage by standing the cut and trimmed stems in deep water for several hours. Finish off the completed bouquet with a large ribbon bow, making it perfectly suited as a presentation bouquet, being comfortable to hold or cradle across the arm. At the end of the evening you can simply drop the arrangement in a vase of water to create an instant display for a central point in the room.

1 *Select the tallest and straightest stems of flowers or foliage to form the central column around which to build the remaining material.*

Clean the ends of the stems of both flowers and foliage before starting to assemble the bouquet.

Graceful sprays of Oncidium Golden Shower dance like clouds of butterflies on wiry, branching sprays.

2 *Lay each stem at a slight angle to the original, turning the bunch slightly with each addition. Gradually build the stems into a spiral with the stems crossing at the same point.*

3 *Mix foliage and flowers together as you build up the spiral. Finish off with some shorter stems of foliage to complete the shape.*

4 *Use a length of ribbon to hold the bouquet together. When complete, wind the ribbon around firmly and secure it without damaging the stems.*

When you cut the stems off level, the bouquet will stand on a flat surface unsupported.

The vibrant red flowers of Renanthera Anne Black *will last for several weeks in water.*

The rich green leaves of Crocosmia *and* Polygonatum *add height, with hosta leaves around the base.*

5 *Complete the bouquet by attaching a generous ribbon bow. Drop this lavish gathering of flowers and foliage into a suitable container for a spectacular but informal display.*

Choose a deep, stable container to drop the flowers into.

131

Paphiopedilums - oriental style

Paphiopedilums have often been described as the most primitive of orchids and, with their long erect stems and single flowers, they make ideal subjects for an oriental-style arrangement. Here we have used a stoneware oven dish, but you could use any type of shallow container to hold this simple but stunning display. The straight lines and angular corners of the dish echo the simple lines of the bamboo, and the colors of both bamboo and dish complete the near perfect harmony of a display that uses just a few flowers. The display is arranged in two pin holders, both firmly secured into the dish with waterproof adhesive strips. In the wild, the stems of most paphiopedilums support their flowers high above the foliage. You can recreate this effect by positioning each flower so that its unusual and distinctive features can be clearly appreciated. The oriental flavor of the display has been emphasized by adding sprays of *Acer palmatum* around the base.

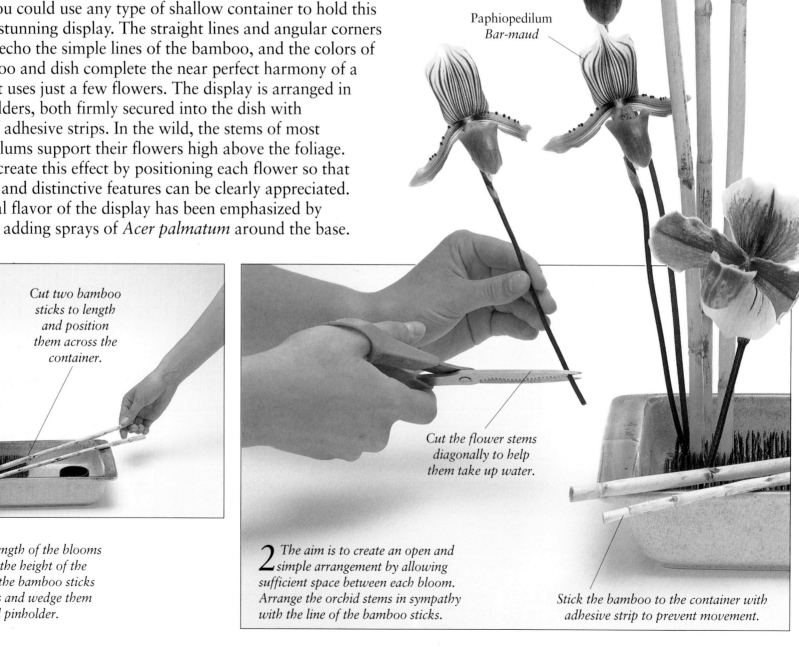

Paphiopedilum
lawrenceanum

Paphiopedilum
Bar-maud

Cut the flower stems
diagonally to help
them take up water.

Stick the bamboo to the container with
adhesive strip to prevent movement.

*Cut two bamboo
sticks to length
and position
them across the
container.*

1 *Consider the length of the blooms when planning the height of the arrangement. Cut the bamboo sticks to different lengths and wedge them into a well-secured pinholder.*

2 *The aim is to create an open and simple arrangement by allowing sufficient space between each bloom. Arrange the orchid stems in sympathy with the line of the bamboo sticks.*

3 *Insert short lengths of foliage into the base of the arrangement to add visual 'weight'. Cover the pinholder to complete the display.*

4 *Fill the dish with water so that the ends of the flowers and foliage are well covered. Notice how the rich green Acer foliage enhances the hint of green in the orchids' sepals and petals.*

Paphiopedilum
*Millionette x
Wendbourne*

Paphiopedilum
barbatum

5 *To create extra interest, place more bamboo sticks in front of the arrangement to soften the lines of the base of the dish and extend the display out into the room.*

133

Cool, green and classic

This arrangement is based on a low, classically decorated bowl with a lipped top that makes it ideal for use with wire mesh as a foundation to hold the flower stems because, once crumpled and fixed in place, the mesh will not move. Although wire mesh seems a little old-fashioned compared with foam, it does have the advantage of holding the stems completely immersed in water; foam tends to lose water relatively quickly and the bottom of the stems could become dry. To emphasize the soft green tones of the orchids, this display is built up around the stark, angular shapes of the unripe seedpods of the common peony-flowered garden poppy. Their dark blue-green color and rigid form act as the 'bones' around which the 'flesh' of the display is constructed. Shorter sprigs of foliage leaves around the base not only act as a foil to the flowers, but also hide the wire mesh from view. The subtle shades of lime green that dominate this display give it a gentle and soothing appeal that would suit both traditional and modern rooms.

3 Working from the center of the display outwards, insert short leaves and sprigs of foliage to cover the wire mesh in the base.

The unripe seedpods on the long, straight stems of the common peony-flowered garden poppy bring an unusual blue-green color to the display.

1 Crumple a piece of plastic-coated wire mesh and push it firmly into the bowl. This will anchor the stems and ensure that they are immersed in water.

Cut the stems cleanly and diagonally to help them take up water.

2 Cut the garden poppy stems to the required lengths and position them in the wire mesh base. Use these to outline the height, width and shape of the arrangement.

Wisteria leaves and the young shoots of heather provide a contrast in form but blend in with the color of the orchids.

Check that the water level covers all the stems and top up the bowl regularly to keep the display fresh.

4 Insert the longest-stemmed orchids carefully through the foliage and into the wire mesh. Select and locate these stems so that they are similar in height and width to the poppy heads already in position.

Use the natural curve of the stems to accentuate the design.

5 Add shorter-stemmed orchid flowers to the center front of the arrangement to develop a central focal point. Make sure that you insert these deep into the container so that they reach well below the water level.

The lime green flowers of Dendrobium Kasam Gold provide a stylish and understated appeal to this arrangement.

6 When you have placed the last of the orchids, complete the arrangement by filling in with foliage where you can see gaps. Remember to fill in the back as well as the front.

A mixed posy bowl

To make this small posy, you will need a bowl or dish that is deep enough to hold a generous reservoir of water in the base. Fix the foam securely into the container using either a foam anchor in the base of the bowl, or tape the block of foam firmly across the top using waterproof florist tape. This delightful little arrangement would be suitable either for a dining or an occasional table, as it can be viewed from all angles. It makes good use of a number of shorter-stemmed orchids in order to create an attractive arrangement whichever direction you look at it. The orchids featured here are in shades of yellows, golds, browns and greens that blend in with the soft tones of the *Nephrolepis* fern. Sprays of *Euonymus* and golden *Marjoram* foliage also add to the warm and pleasing appearance of the display.

Use a block of foam large enough to be raised well above the rim of the bowl.

1 *Secure well-soaked flower foam with florist tape, making sure that the end of the tape is fixed to the bowl. Pull the tape tightly over the foam to hold it firmly in the dish.*

2 *First create the overall shape of the design with ferns and other foliage. Turn the dish as you work so that you can view it from all sides.*

3 *Continue to build up the shape of the posy by adding more foliage. Finally, add the flowers, carefully pushing the stems into the wet foam.*

This stem of fern determines the finished height of the arrangement.

Paphiopedilum
gratrixianum, *with its
soft golden tones,
stands proudly at the
apex of the posy.*

*The large-lipped,
chestnut-spotted,
yellow hybrid
Odontocidium* Tiger
Hambühren.

5 *When completed, this delightful
mixed posy will continue to give
you pleasure for a considerable time.
If one of the orchids fades, simply
replace it and in this way you will
maintain the posy's fresh appearance.*

Single stems of Lycaste
Luciana *last well as a
cut flower in this type
of arrangement.*

4 *Fill the container with water. To
keep the flowers and foliage in
good condition, spray them regularly
with a fine mist sprayer. They will
respond well to this type
of treatment.*

Odontoglossum
Rialto x Odontioda
Pacific Gold

*The short
stems of
Dendrobium
Montrose
AM/RHS are
just long
enough to be
pushed into
the foam.*

Cymbidium *Indian Tea,
an early hybrid.*

137

Orchids with glass beads

Flower foam or chicken wire would be quite inappropriate materials for a modern arrangement in a square glass container such as this. Instead, glass beads have been chosen to hold the small number of flower stems firmly in position. Their soft green coloring plays an important part in creating a balance to the whole display. Place the glass beads into the container until it is approximately two-thirds full. If the orchids are tall and top heavy, you may need to add more beads to give the stems support. Several hours before starting the arrangement, condition the flowers and foliage by cutting the ends of the stems with a diagonal cut and standing them in deep water. Just two types of orchid make up this display. The rose-purple lip of the *Vanda tricolor* blends perfectly with the strong solid color of the *Masdevallia coccinea* to produce a stunning arrangement that is ideally suited to a modern setting. The central focal point has been created with just three *Hosta* leaves.

Glass beads are an alternative means of holding flower stems in position, particularly when just a few stems need supporting.

1 *Fill the vase until it is approximately two-thirds full of beads. Pour some water over the beads to moisten them and to make inserting the stems a smoother operation.*

2 *Push the flower stems as deep as possible into the beads to ensure that they are firmly gripped in place and well below the eventual water level.*

3 *Arrange three solid-green hosta leaves around the stems of the Vanda tricolor to create a focal point for this striking display.*

4 *Take care when pushing thin-stemmed flowers, such as this Masdevallia, into the glass beads. They are easily bent or broken.*

Vanda tricolor suavis *is a native of Java and was introduced into cultivation in 1846. It has heavily scented fleshy flowers.*

The most unusual waxy flowers of Masdevallia coccinea sway on their wiry stems when exposed to the slightest movement of air.

5 *Add water to just below the level of the glass beads. Do not be tempted to incorporate too many flowers or an excess of foliage, which will only spoil the dramatic effect created by the strong colors and simplicity of the display.*

A basket of dendrobiums

A small bowl filled with foam and securely anchored into this wide, flat basket with an arching, hooplike handle allows you to create a sumptuous arrangement, with the illusion of flowers piled up and spilling gracefully out over the sides of the basket. Basketware for flower arranging has become increasingly popular over the years and this display, being long and low and having an all-round appeal, would be perfect as the centerpiece for a dining table. By lifting it with one finger under the handle, you can easily and safely transfer it to an occasional or coffee table in another room. Before beginning any arrangement, carefully condition both flowers and foliage to extend their life as much as possible so that you can gain the best value from them. Cut the stems diagonally, exposing the maximum amount of cut area to the water. You may need to bruise the woody foliage stems with a hammer. Stand flowers and foliage in deep water in a cool place for several hours. Once this arrangement is complete, keep a careful eye on it; as the bowl in the basket is comparatively small and shallow, you must regularly top it up with fresh water.

3 *Starting with the longest ones, insert the flower stems over the edge of the bowl, pushing them deep into the foam so that the flowers rest gently on the foliage.*

As you reach the center of the basket, slightly increase the angle at which you push the flowers into the foam so that they become more vertical.

The handle should be strong enough to enable you to lift up the finished arrangement.

Press the container firmly onto two lengths of adhesive strip.

1 *Cut a block of well-soaked foam to fit the container, but standing about 1in(2.5cm) above the rim. Secure the foam into the bowl with crossed lengths of florist tape.*

2 *Make use of the natural curves of the stems and allow the foliage to languish lazily over the bottom and sides of the basket.*

Keep the handle of the basket a major feature of the design and do not completely obscure it with flowers.

Reviving wilted flowers

Flowers of the phalaenopsis type of dendrobium, imported in vast numbers from the Far East and used in this and several other displays in this book, may well arrive in a very soft, limp condition, particularly if they have traveled a long distance out of water. You can revive them perfectly by cutting about 0.5in(1.25cm) off the end of the stems and totally immersing the blooms in a bath of cold water. After about 30 minutes, the flowers become quite revived and are not damaged by the water. Stand them in deep water for several hours and condition as usual.

4 Continue building up the sides into a mound, keeping within the confines of the handle. Use the minimum amount of foliage, as the flowers should expand from deep inside the arrangement.

These pale green buds will open into the pure white flowers of the hybrid Dendrobium Big White.

Dendrobium *Bom*

Solid dark green leaves of Pulmonaria saccharata.

141

Paphiopedilums with shells

Placing shells in a clear glass bowl adds a considerable amount of interest to what is a very simple arrangement of just five flowers, all of the same species. The shells with their varied shapes, colors and textures not only add decorative interest within the bowl, but they also secure the foam in a central position and form a base for the arrangements. The foliage should not cover too much of the shells or the rim of the glass bowl. Arrange it carefully so that it seems to emerge from a central point within the bowl and, together with the orchids, appears to 'erupt' like a volcano. When complete, this charming arrangement shows off the paphiopedilums' dramatic shape to great effect. Often called the 'lady's slipper orchid', the paphiopedilums' subtle shades of color make them unique, even among other orchids. The flowers featured in this display are *Paphiopedilum barbatum*, a species from the Malay Peninsula and first introduced into cultivation in 1840.

Before inserting foliage into the foam, remove any side branches or leaves that would sit below the water level. This is a sprig of Buxus (box).

2 Push individual leaves into the foam, taking care that they do not cover or spill over the rim of the bowl or hide the seashells from view.

The thin, clear glass allows an uninterrupted view of the shells.

1 Place a small block of wet foam in the center of the bowl and hold it firmly in place with an assortment of shells of various shapes and colors.

3 *Select each flower carefully, bearing in mind the angle from which it will be seen. Arrange some in profile to show off their unusual form.*

4 *Use the flowerheads of Alchemilla mollis to provide a contrasting texture. Foliage material is just as important as good-quality blooms.*

5 *Add water until the bowl is approximately two-thirds full. Top up the water level regularly and, given an occasional spray with a fine mist sprayer, the arrangement should last for two to three weeks.*

To appreciate the subtle colors in this display, stand it against a plain background.

Add sufficient Alchemilla mollis to form a link between the individual leaves around the foam in the base of the container and the flowers and foliage above it.

The species Paphiopedilum barbatum normally has one flower per stem, but occasionally two.

143

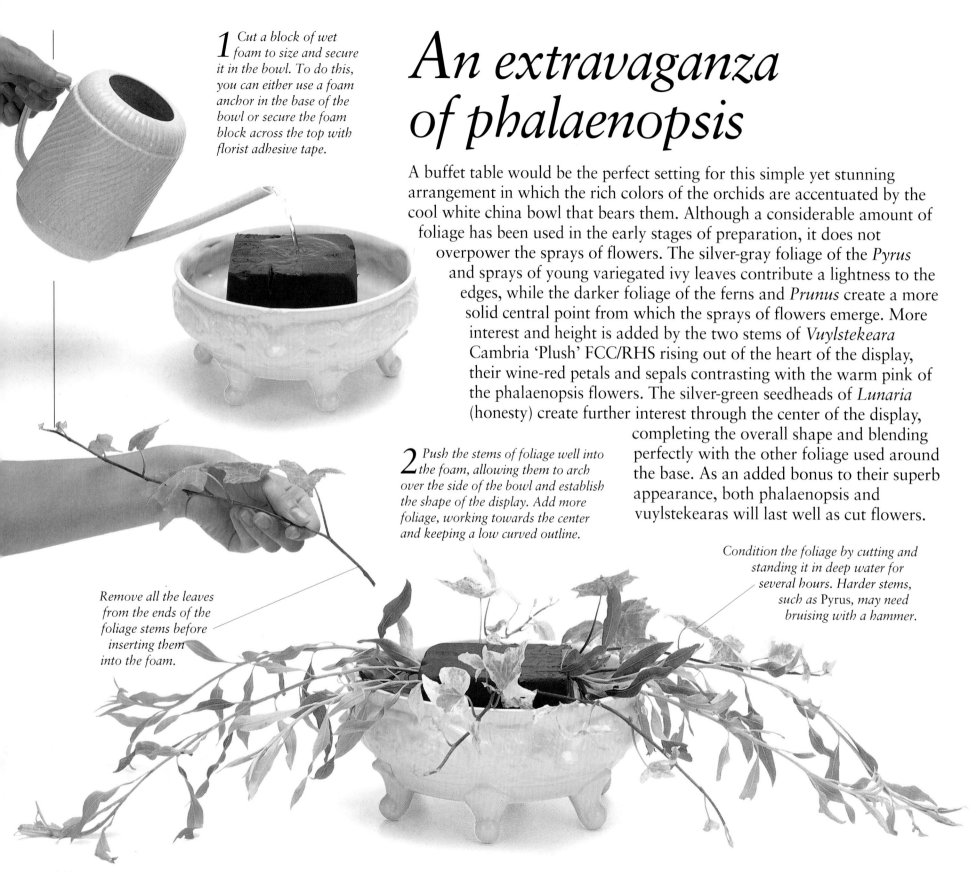

1 *Cut a block of wet foam to size and secure it in the bowl. To do this, you can either use a foam anchor in the base of the bowl or secure the foam block across the top with florist adhesive tape.*

An extravaganza of phalaenopsis

A buffet table would be the perfect setting for this simple yet stunning arrangement in which the rich colors of the orchids are accentuated by the cool white china bowl that bears them. Although a considerable amount of foliage has been used in the early stages of preparation, it does not overpower the sprays of flowers. The silver-gray foliage of the *Pyrus* and sprays of young variegated ivy leaves contribute a lightness to the edges, while the darker foliage of the ferns and *Prunus* create a more solid central point from which the sprays of flowers emerge. More interest and height is added by the two stems of *Vuylstekeara* Cambria 'Plush' FCC/RHS rising out of the heart of the display, their wine-red petals and sepals contrasting with the warm pink of the phalaenopsis flowers. The silver-green seedheads of *Lunaria* (honesty) create further interest through the center of the display, completing the overall shape and blending perfectly with the other foliage used around the base. As an added bonus to their superb appearance, both phalaenopsis and vuylstekearas will last well as cut flowers.

2 *Push the stems of foliage well into the foam, allowing them to arch over the side of the bowl and establish the shape of the display. Add more foliage, working towards the center and keeping a low curved outline.*

Remove all the leaves from the ends of the foliage stems before inserting them into the foam.

Condition the foliage by cutting and standing it in deep water for several hours. Harder stems, such as Pyrus, *may need bruising with a hammer.*

3 Hold the stems of the phalaenopsis roughly in position before cutting them, so that when you push them into the foam they will arch over but not touch the table.

Cut the stems diagonally to give the maximum surface area in contact with the water.

4 Complete the arched effect by placing shorter stems towards the center. The wine-colored vuylstekearas bursting from the center make a dramatic impact.

Tall spikes of Vuylstekeara Cambria 'Plush' FCC/RHS.

Honesty seedheads

These candy pink flowers of Phalaenopsis *Pink Chief x Fairvale* are perfectly spaced along the stem.

Handle the delicate phalaenopsis flowers with care, as they are easily bruised.

Phalaenopsis *Pink Chief x Zuma Cupid.*

5 Sprays of Lunaria seedheads act as a foil to the tall vuylstekeara spikes. Fill in the area around the top of the bowl with foliage, taking care not to obscure the phalaenopsis.

Magenta magic

This sumptuous and boldly colored arrangement is based on a round china vase with a raised base that provides sufficient height for the flowers to flow down gracefully to the surface of the table. In addition, the bowl is generous enough to hold an ample amount of water and is the ideal shape to contain a mound of wire mesh to support the flower stems. At first sight, this display may seem extravagant in its use of flowers, but as an all-round arrangement destined to feature as the centerpiece on a large dining table, its striking appearance more than justifies its lavish use of ingredients. Do remember to keep the vase topped up with water, and an occasional spray with a fine mist sprayer will maintain the flowers at the peak of freshness. Before spraying, always move arrangements away from polished furniture to avoid marking the surface.

1 Crumple the plastic-coated wire mesh into a ball the same size as the container, squeezing it into the bowl to create as tight a fit as possible.

2 Pass florist waterproof adhesive tape through the mesh and use it to stretch the wire to the edge of the vase before taping it securely into place.

It is much easier to secure the wire mesh in position if you use a vase with a slightly lipped rim.

4 Continue building foliage in towards the center, leaving it quite open at this stage to allow easy access for the flower stems. Notice how the contrasting shapes of the foliage create an interest in their own right.

3 Begin by placing foliage around the rim, carefully concealing any tape used to secure the wire. Turn the vase continually as you work to help you create a good balanced shape.

Leave the stems of foliage long enough to penetrate deep into the vase.

A mound of wire is helpful when you insert stems that are to fall over the rim.

The small flower buds on the ends of these sprays of orchids are unlikely to open.

6 Space out the lacy flowerheads of Aegopodium, or ground elder, to resemble starbursts highlighted against a deep purple sky.

The deep magenta flowers of Dendrobium *Madame Pompadour.*

Foliage for impact

It is impossible to overemphasize the importance of foliage in flower arranging and in this book you can see how different types of foliage create different effects. It can form part of the display, act as a foil to the flowers, add weight to a display or make it light and airy, or simply serve to hide the mechanics of the support material. Whatever role it is to fill, choose it as carefully as you would the flowers, making sure it is clean and fresh. Cut the stems diagonally or, if they are hard and woody, bruise them with a hammer. Make sure they have a good long drink before using them in an arrangement.

5 *Allow the natural curves of the flower stems to flow gracefully out from the sides of the display. Space the blooms sufficiently far apart so that you can see each one clearly in the final arrangement.*

In contrast to the magenta flowers of the older hybrid Dendrobium *Madame Pompadour,* the more modern, larger flowers of Dendrobium *Sabeen* have a richer, warmer color and a velvety texture.

The large, white-edged leaves of Hosta decorata *and the mottled green of* Syngonium *provide a fitting background for this striking orchid arrangement.*

Sprigs of the small green leaves of common box and Euonymus *separate the stems of orchids and fill in the gaps.*

147

A living basket of orchids

Ficus benjamina

To many orchid lovers, cutting flowers to use them in an arrangement in the home would be quite alien. However, sharing their beauty as plants assembled into an attractive living display seems to make much more sense. The vibrant golden shades of this generously filled basket would lift the mood of any dark corner, or could be used to create a centerpiece for a dormant fireplace during the summer. With the exception of the *Masdevallia urosalpinx* peering over the rim of the basket, the orchids used in this display are all from the family Oncidiinae. The two taller orchids are excellent examples of training flower spikes with the minimum amount of support, allowing the stems to arch over and display their flowers to full advantage. Using a water-retentive aggregate in the bottom of the basket helps to increase the amount of moisture in the air around the plants and greatly reduce the risk of them suffering from the dry conditions usually found in the home. Keep this aggregate layer moist and spray the plants occasionally with a fine mist sprayer to maintain the display at a peak of freshness.

These expanded clay granules are ideal for creating a water-retaining layer in the base.

1 *Choose a deep wicker basket with an integral plastic lining and add sufficient moistened aggregate to form a humid 'microclimate' and raise the pots to a suitable level.*

2 *Settle the background foliage plant down firmly on the aggregate and position orchid plants with tall stems around it, working from the back of basket towards the front.*

3 *Before finally setting any plants into the display, it is a good idea to offer each one into its approximate position, then turn the plant first one way then the other to judge from which angle it looks best.*

The delicate flowers of Oncidium Gower Ramsey arch gracefully on springy stems.

A well-grown plant of Odonticidium *Rupella*, partially supported then allowed to arch over naturally.

6 Use small ferns or moss to finish off the arrangement by covering the tops of the pots. The basket handle not only adds to the appearance of the display, but also makes it easy to move.

4 *Avoid a top-heavy look by using some shorter orchids. These will need supporting to allow their flowers to peer over the rim of the basket.*

Rossioglossum williamsoni

The gaily colored Rossioglossum grande *from Guatemala, affectionately known as the 'clown orchid' from the manlike structure in the center of the flower.*

5 *An occasional light spray with a fine mist sprayer is very beneficial to the orchids in the dry conditions of the home. This will not harm the foliage plants used in this display.*

Masdevallia urosalpinx

A young plant of Odonticidium *Tiger Hambühren.*

Orchids with a twist

Using dried grasses, seedpods and cones to echo the natural colors of basketware containers creates a study in shapes and textures, accentuated by the natural ramblings of a twisted hazel branch. The subtle shades of the dried materials call for an orchid with colors that are not strident but which blend harmoniously with the dried elements, producing a simple but lovely design with enormous appeal. Sprays of the very long-lasting *Arachnis* Maggie 'Ouei', commonly known as the spider orchid, appear to be pushing their way out through the display, all springing from one point deep within the basket. Placing the arrangement on a shallow basketware tray adds considerably to the general proportions of the display as well as further reflecting the subtle shades of the orchids. Scattering a few cones on the tray, similar to those used in the arrangement, also helps to link all the elements together. The arachnis is an orchid most suited to being used as a cut flower and, providing you keep the container topped up with water, it will last for a very long time in perfect condition.

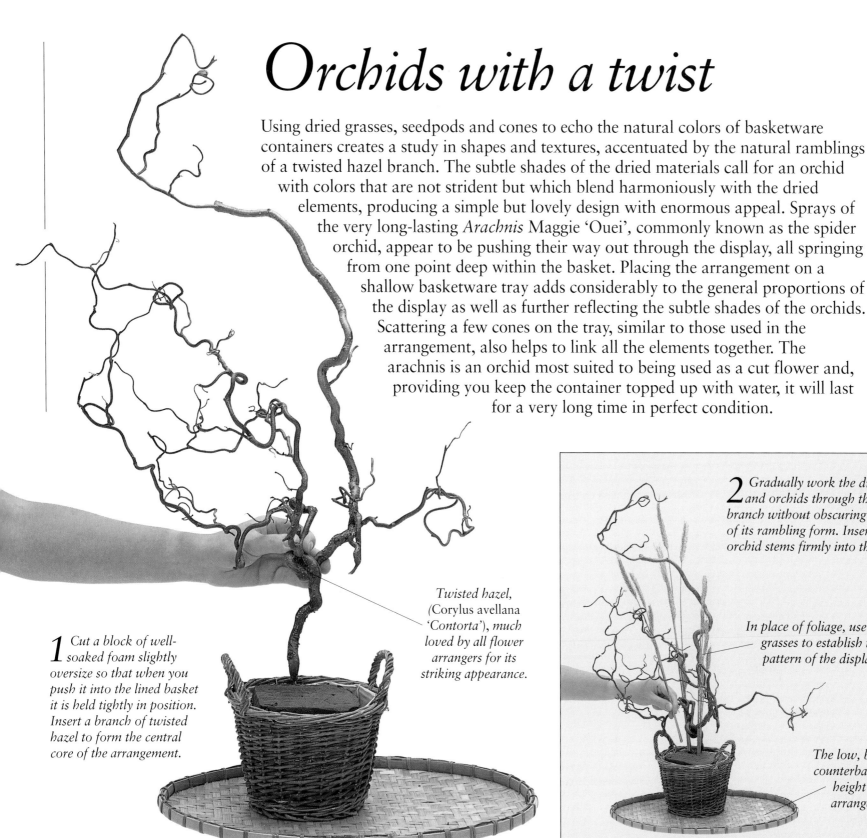

2 *Gradually work the dried grasses and orchids through the hazel branch without obscuring too much of its rambling form. Insert the orchid stems firmly into the foam.*

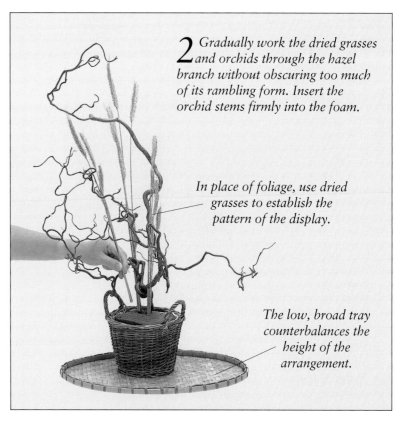

In place of foliage, use dried grasses to establish the pattern of the display.

The low, broad tray counterbalances the height of the arrangement.

*Twisted hazel, (*Corylus avellana *'Contorta'), much loved by all flower arrangers for its striking appearance.*

1 *Cut a block of well-soaked foam slightly oversize so that when you push it into the lined basket it is held tightly in position. Insert a branch of twisted hazel to form the central core of the arrangement.*

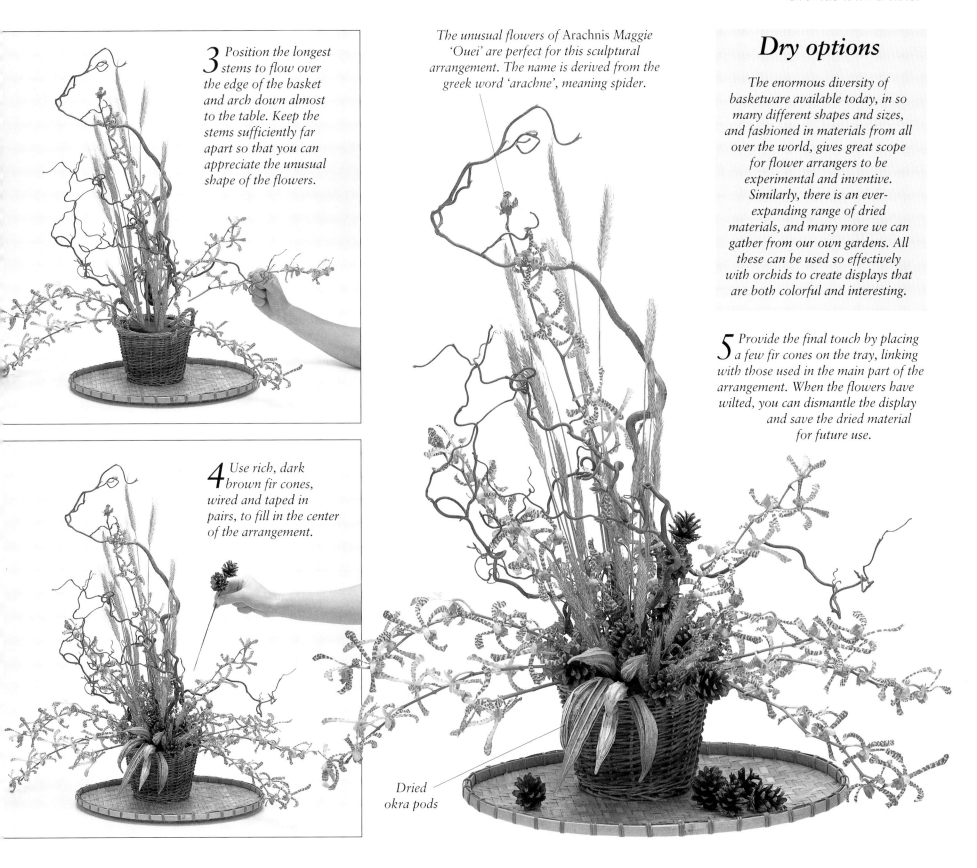

3 Position the longest stems to flow over the edge of the basket and arch down almost to the table. Keep the stems sufficiently far apart so that you can appreciate the unusual shape of the flowers.

4 Use rich, dark brown fir cones, wired and taped in pairs, to fill in the center of the arrangement.

The unusual flowers of Arachnis Maggie 'Ouei' are perfect for this sculptural arrangement. The name is derived from the greek word 'arachne', meaning spider.

Dry options

The enormous diversity of basketware available today, in so many different shapes and sizes, and fashioned in materials from all over the world, gives great scope for flower arrangers to be experimental and inventive. Similarly, there is an ever-expanding range of dried materials, and many more we can gather from our own gardens. All these can be used so effectively with orchids to create displays that are both colorful and interesting.

5 Provide the final touch by placing a few fir cones on the tray, linking with those used in the main part of the arrangement. When the flowers have wilted, you can dismantle the display and save the dried material for future use.

Dried okra pods

An orchid-filled hamper

Many items around the home make suitable containers in which to build living displays of orchid plants. This wicker hamper is an excellent choice, being deep and square. Do make sure that it does not suffer from water damage by lining it with a double layer of plastic sheeting. Using a water-retentive aggregate in the bottom of the hamper will act as a safeguard against overwatering and help to produce a humid micro-climate more acceptable to the plants. The care taken to train, stake and tie the flower spikes as they grow will be rewarded when they come into bloom; staking the spikes very rigidly will produce a stiff, unnatural look, whereas insufficient tying will produce plants too ungainly to be used. The plants displayed here work together to provide a well-balanced and pleasing arrangement.

3 *Use bold foliage plants as a background to the orchids. This not only adds depth, but also improves the overall impact of the group.*

Ficus benjamina

1 *Select a container deep enough to allow the pots to sit inside and be hidden from view. Line it with a double thickness of plastic to form a waterproof tray.*

2 *Cover the base with a layer of aggregate to allow good drainage and also act as a moisture tray to maintain humidity.*

Secure the lid of the hamper in an open position before planting.

152

4 *Select the position of each plant, with tall spikes at the center back and shorter arching ones to the front and sides.*

5 *Raise shallow pots by adding more stones to bring their flowers up into the required position or stand them on upturned pots or blocks of wood .*

Vuylstekeara
Cambria 'Plush'
AM/RHS

6 *Conceal the pots from view by dropping in small ferns or other foliage plants. Alternatively, placing decorative moss will have the same effect of finishing off the group.*

Odontioda
cooksonii x
Wilsonara
Lyoth Ruby

Dancing flowers of the pansy orchid Miltonia *Limelight.*

Masdevallia
coccinea x
trochilus

Masdevallia
infracta

Small Nephrolepis
ferns dropped in to conceal the pots.

Oncidium
Puch

Rich and romantic pinks and reds

The rich burgundies, crimsons and pinks of clematis flowers combine wonderfully well with many summer flowers, including lilies, roses, dianthus and honeysuckle. They provide strong, simple shapes and splashes of solid color, and add texture and richness to any arrangement. For maximum impact, use clematis combined with other blooms in a saturated mix of one color without any contrast or even green foliage. Here, the flowers have been arranged into a rustic wooden bowl with an interesting surface finish that makes them look even richer.

The display includes several different types of clematis, some large-flowered and some small, but they are all in the same color key, from a pale, subtle, grayish pink to deepest velvety maroon. Choose garden flowers to go with the clematis if you have them, such as old-fashioned roses, dianthus and carnations, and add a few exotic pink lilies for their magnificent perfume and stunning shape and color.

4 Cut pieces of foam to fit inside the bowl and soak them in water. Follow the manufacturer's timing for this. Pack them tightly together in the center of the bowl.

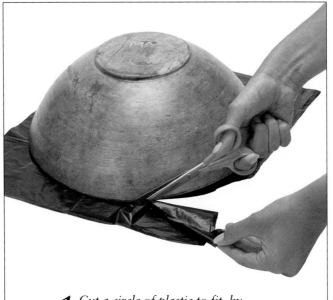

1 Cut a circle of plastic to fit, by cutting around the edge of the upturned bowl. An old plastic bag is perfectly suitable for this purpose.

2 Turn the bowl the right way up and put the plastic in place. The plastic protects the bowl and retains the water around the arrangement.

3 Push the plastic down inside the wooden bowl and smooth it out evenly all round. Obviously it will be somewhat smaller than the bowl, but this is how it is intended to be.

5 Begin to put areas of flowers into the foam, working from one side to the other. This gives a strong look, rather than dotting the flowers all over.

6 Continue adding flowers to the arrangement, aiming to create a curved, dome-shaped outline above the bowl. This arrangement is designed to be seen from all round.

'Comtesse de Bouchaud' is a pale and pretty pink.

Clematis texensis 'Etoile Rose' has thickly textured, bell-shaped flowers that hang down.

Clematis 'General Sikorski'

Mist the whole arrangement occasionally with a fine spray of water.

7 The finished arrangement would look lovely on a low table or as a centerpiece, particularly against a background of dark, polished wood.

155

A midsummer mixture

Clematis have a particular way of growing and flowering in the garden. It is best to try to recreate this when making indoor arrangements, rather than forcing the flowers to do something else. This stemmed dish allows the large flowerheads to look quite natural and some can even tumble down to the surface below, as if they were still growing. The rich mix of colors and profusion of blooms makes a spectacular arrangement for any position in the house. Leaving some of the foliage amongst the flowers on the stem provides color contrast and a change of shape and texture, which helps to define the different varieties that have been used. This arrangement is ideal when plenty of flower types are blooming at the same time in midsummer, giving you the opportunity to pick a range of clematis in shades of mauve, purple and burgundy. You could also use a glass cake stand for this idea or even balance a dish or plate on something else to create the same attractive tiered effect.

This clematis is the pale mauve-pink 'Hagley Hybrid'.

1 *Flower foam must be soaked to be really effective. Hold it under the water until it sinks to the bottom. Cut a piece of the wet foam to fit the dish.*

2 *Place the foam in the center of the dish and secure it with special florist's tape designed to work with damp foam. In this case one strip is enough, but add more pieces if you wish.*

There is room to top up the dish with extra water if needed; the lip will stop it overflowing.

3 *Put the first blooms in place, working at the base of the foam and around the display. Consider the angle from which the flowers will be seen.*

Clematis for cutting

Late-flowering, small-flowered clematis seem less likely to wilt once cut, whereas the early-flowering, very large-headed blooms are trickier. Many varieties are particularly suitable for cutting. Some good ones to try are: Pink: 'Dr. Ruppel' and 'Etoile Rose'. Purple: 'The President' and 'Lasurstern'. Mauve: 'Barbara Jackman' and 'Marcel Moser'. Light blue: 'General Sikorski' and 'H.F. Young'. White: 'Moonlight'.

The tumbling foliage adds to the natural effect.

To achieve a lighter finished effect, do not entirely obscure the stem of the dish with blooms.

4 *The finished arrangement looks elegant and stylish. The fact that it is so simple is not obvious at all, but it does rely on perfect blooms at the peak of condition. Stand it out of full sun and enjoy it for several days.*

Clematis with sweet honeysuckle

Many of the small-flowered clematis varieties are very suitable for cut flower arrangements and seem to last well in water. Most types bloom from late summer onwards and their lightness and delicacy makes for elegant and stylish designs. In many cases they are easier to use than the very large-headed blooms, which are mostly seen in early summer. Combining them with other flowers or foliage gives you the chance to introduce contrasting colors, flower shapes and textures. Very few clematis varieties have scent except some of the small-flowered species types, so this arrangement mixes the pretty purple *Clematis* x *eriostemon* with a highly scented, pale lemon honeysuckle called 'Graham Thomas'. It is a suitable combination that might just as easily be found in the summer garden, scrambling over a low wall or pergola. The small-flowered types of clematis grow with a mass of flowerheads all together, so it is easiest to pick them in a large trailing piece, with many flowers and buds attached. If the plant is thriving, there will be plenty of stems that can be spared for the house. You can, of course, pick individual blooms, too, for much smaller scale arrangements if you do not want to take much material from the plant.

Once cut, the trails of clematis are prettiest arranged very naturally as if they are still growing. A tall, funnel-shaped, clear glass vase makes a light and delicate container for the clematis. The shape of the vase makes arranging very simple, as the flowers can fan out naturally and form a good rounded shape at the top. Split the thick ends of the cut stems a little way up their length to allow water to be taken up easily. If you do not have a honeysuckle to use with the clematis, you could use any pale or golden yellow flower or shrub, such as solidago, coreopsis, achillea or even yellow roses.

1 First sort out the flowers and separate out the two types, the clematis and the honeysuckle. Recut their stems at a slanting angle. Fill the vase with water.

Use freshly drawn, cool water to give the flowers a good start. Make sure that the vase is clean.

2 Trim away any lower leaves on the stems of honeysuckle, using your fingers or secateurs if you find it easier. Leave a few small leaves at the base of the clematis stems.

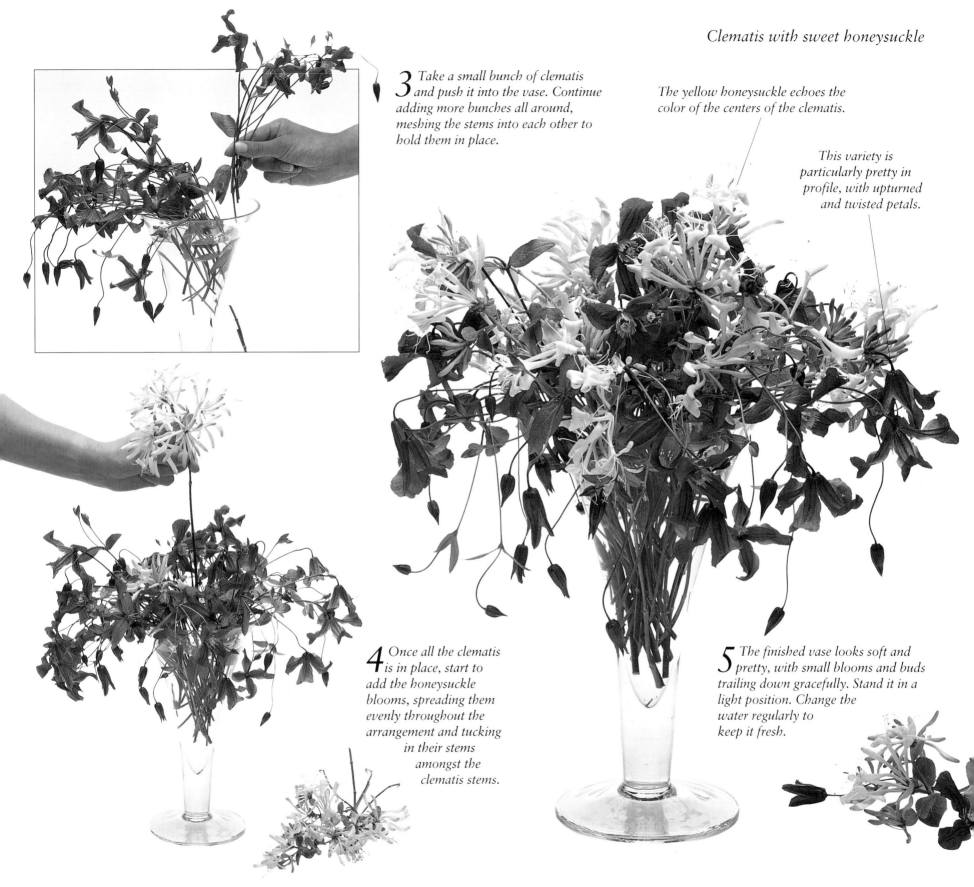

3 Take a small bunch of clematis and push it into the vase. Continue adding more bunches all around, meshing the stems into each other to hold them in place.

The yellow honeysuckle echoes the color of the centers of the clematis.

This variety is particularly pretty in profile, with upturned and twisted petals.

4 Once all the clematis is in place, start to add the honeysuckle blooms, spreading them evenly throughout the arrangement and tucking in their stems amongst the clematis stems.

5 The finished vase looks soft and pretty, with small blooms and buds trailing down gracefully. Stand it in a light position. Change the water regularly to keep it fresh.

A late summer classic arrangement

Clematis can be used in the most classical kinds of flower arrangements with great success. Their trailing stems and foliage add interest to more solid flower shapes. There are only a few yellow clematis species, but they are amongst some of the most decorative types and include the pretty *Clematis tangutica* and the subtle, tiny-flowered *Clematis rehderiana*, both used in this arrangement. *C. tangutica* has thick, lemon peel-like petals and small ferny foliage, while *C. rehderiana* has miniature bell-shaped, pale yellowy cream flowers in clusters and smells sweetly of cowslips. Both bloom through late summer onwards. Pick whole pieces of the climbing stem to use for cut flowers or use just single stems of flowers for miniature arrangements. Here the yellows have been mixed with brilliant scarlet crocosmia, nasturtiums and yellow lilies for a spectacular explosion of late summer color.

4 *Now begin to add the larger flowers, such as the yellow lilies, and fill in with nasturtiums and their leaves. A few stems of fennel flowers are also included.*

1 *This classic black vase needs some wire netting to hold the flower stems in place. Cut a piece slightly larger than the neck of the vase and crumple it slightly.*

2 *Put a block of damp flower foam into the vase so that it protrudes slightly. Push the netting over the foam; tuck the edges under the neck of the vase.*

3 *Start by putting a few large pieces of foliage and the stems of crocosmia in place to establish the overall size and shape of the finished arrangement.*

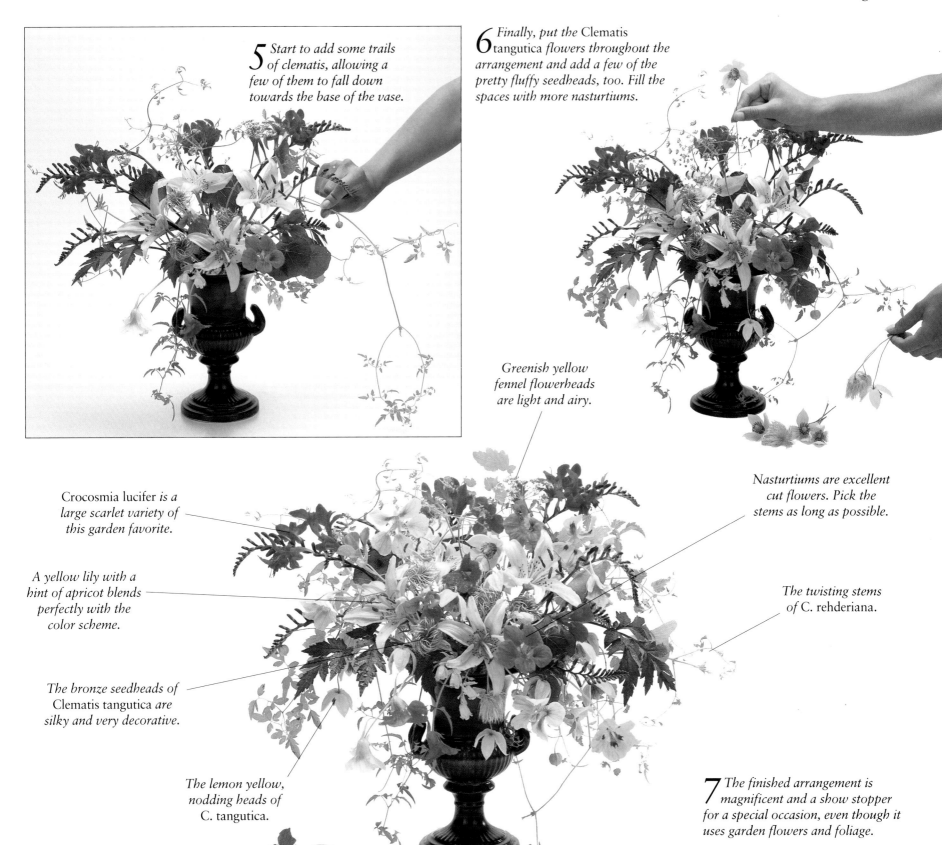

5 *Start to add some trails of clematis, allowing a few of them to fall down towards the base of the vase.*

6 *Finally, put the* Clematis tangutica *flowers throughout the arrangement and add a few of the pretty fluffy seedheads, too. Fill the spaces with more nasturtiums.*

Greenish yellow fennel flowerheads are light and airy.

Nasturtiums are excellent cut flowers. Pick the stems as long as possible.

Crocosmia lucifer *is a large scarlet variety of this garden favorite.*

A yellow lily with a hint of apricot blends perfectly with the color scheme.

The twisting stems of C. rehderiana.

The bronze seedheads of Clematis tangutica *are silky and very decorative.*

The lemon yellow, nodding heads of C. tangutica.

7 *The finished arrangement is magnificent and a show stopper for a special occasion, even though it uses garden flowers and foliage.*

A country basket of purple and green

Different varieties of clematis mix well together in flower arrangements, and choosing shades of one single color creates a harmonious and pleasing effect. In this display, the acid green of *Alchemilla mollis* has been added to form a contrast that throws the deep purples and mauves of the clematis into relief. The alchemilla flowers also make a good filling material between the clematis flowers, so that they do not have to be crammed too tightly together to fill the space.

Baskets are excellent containers for simple country arrangements and the texture of plaited twigs is always effective in complementing the flowers. Of course, if the basket is not already lined like this one, you will have to line it to make it waterproof, as this arrangement relies on a block of flower foam to hold the stems secure. The display is designed to be seen from all round and slightly from above, so the finished basket would look good on any low table, on a windowsill or as a centerpiece.

4 Once the foam is totally covered, tuck the sweet pea blooms in amongst the alchemilla, spacing them out and working evenly all round the basket .

1 Cut sufficient blocks of flower foam to fill the base of the basket. Make sure that they are thoroughly soaked in water before using them. Follow the maker's instructions.

2 Arrange the foam in a basket lined with plastic or aluminum foil to contain any moisture. Some baskets come ready lined.

3 Start by putting stems of alchemilla across the entire area of foam to make a contrasting background for the clematis.

5 *Next, put some of the clematis blooms into the foam, along with a few sprigs of hardy geranium. Mix the light and dark shades of clematis equally throughout the basket.*

6 *Finally, add some sprigs of fresh, deep purple lavender to fill in any large areas of alchemilla that are not interrupted by other flowers.*

A deep burgundy sweet pea mixes well with the other flowers.

7 *The finished basket looks natural and relaxed, with a few stems spilling out beyond the edges. It includes an interesting and varied mixture of flowers and foliage.*

Rich mauve 'General Sikorski' clematis.

Lime green Alchemilla mollis is used as a filler.

A double purple variety of hardy geranium.

Fresh, scented lavender adds a different dimension.

Pink clematis. 'Charisma'

Mixed clematis in a verdigris vase

This small-scale and quite dainty arrangement would be very suitable for a small table, a mantlepiece or any piece of furniture. It is fairly formal in style, because of the elegant, verdigris-finished pottery vase. The narrowness of this vase determines how much material you can put in it, but as the stems of clematis are so thin, it is still possible to fit many different flowers inside without making the display look top-heavy or becoming unstable. To enable you to control where the flowers are positioned, fit a narrow piece of foam into the neck of the vase so that it protrudes a little way above the top edge. Keep an eye on the water level in a vase as small as this, and top it up daily, as the flowers will quickly draw moisture out of the foam. Most of the clematis used here are small-flowered, but there are a few larger ones for interest. A few stems of fresh lavender provide the finishing touch; their spikes contrast well with the softer and flatter clematis blooms.

4 *When you have finished putting all the flowers of the first type of clematis in place, you can begin to add a different variety. Here, pink flowers are mixed in between the purple ones.*

1 *Use a sharp knife to cut a small piece of flower foam to fit the neck of the vase. Soak the foam in water until it is thoroughly wet. Always follow the maker's instructions on preparing the foam for use.*

2 *Push the piece of foam firmly into place, leaving a small amount above the edge of the vase. This adds a little more height to the finished arrangement.*

3 *Start to put one type of clematis into place, spacing the stems out evenly all over the foam. Their height will set the limit to the outline of the arrangement.*

5 When the small clematis are used up, begin to put a few larger flowers in amongst them. For the best effect, do not use more than six to eight larger blooms.

6 Lastly, put in some spikes of fresh lavender, arranging them throughout the display, so that they fill any spaces between the various clematis flowers.

Deep burgundy Clematis *'Niobe' is rich and velvety.*

Clematis *x* durandii, *a good, deep purple clematis for cutting.*

Fresh lavender adds more variety to the arrangement.

Deep mauve Clematis *'Prinz Hendrick' has strong stems that are suitable for cutting.*

Long-lasting Clematis *'Etoile Rose' is an excellent cut flower.*

7 The finished display is neat and compact and densely packed with color and texture. The lavender adds a little scent, as well as welcome contrasting shapes, to the arrangement.

Everyday displays

However busy you are, a simple flower arrangement or two makes a big difference to how a house looks and feels. Try to find time to put together a quick bunch of cheerful flowers for a kitchen table and something welcoming in the hall or living room. These arrangements need not be elaborate, but should provide a splash of color - something fresh and alive - and if possible add the bonus of a delicious scent. For the simplest arrangements, you need just a clean glass vase filled with fresh water, but look out for jugs and bowls that will make pretty, colorful or unusual containers.

Above: *Roses always make extravagant and beautiful arrangements. During the summer there are plenty of garden varieties to choose from, but florists roses are available all year round. Here, pale shell-pink roses and lacy umbellifer flowers echo the colors and design on the beautiful china.*

Left: *A pink luster bowl sets off sugar-pink roses and paler pink spray carnations to perfection. Start by putting gray-green eucalyptus foliage all over damp foam or crumpled wire. Add the spray carnations and then fill the spaces with roses, making a nice curved outline above the top of the bowl.*

Right: *A delicate and lacy mixture of blue love-in-a-mist, anemones, Michaelmas daisies and rue foliage simply arranged in a stemmed glass goblet - perfect for a bedside table, dressing table, or any small space. It is important to keep arrangements in scale with their surroundings - and to choose containers that are in tune with the flowers you put in them, in size as well as in style and color. A delicate display such as this would look quite out of place in a boldly colored pottery vase, for example.*

Below: *Anemones and annual gypsophila in a simple cream vase bring a breath of spring to a kitchen or bathroom windowsill. Remember to change the water regularly.*

Left: *The simplest arrangements are often the most effective. Here, a deep green, glossy jug holds a sunshine yellow mixture of ornamental chillies, alstroemeria, helichrysums, chrysanthemums and roses, all set off by green and yellow gourds.*

Eucalyptus leaves reflect the color of the jug and the gourds around the base.

The strong shape of the ornamental chillies make a bold contrast with the flowers and foliage.

Above: *This small wooden box has been filled with a mixture of garden pansies and violas standing in water inside glass jars hidden in the box. To save space you can put a small group of flowers into a foam base on a waterproof tray, instead of a vase.*

168

Gerbera flowers make a strong impact on their own.

Right: *The stark simplicity of a black glass vase contrasts with the deep golden yellow of ornamental chillies, some carefully positioned chrysanthemum heads and bright orange rosehips. A few pieces of bear grass (Dasylirion) make graphic curving lines out of the arrangement.*

Below: *Pale apricot tulips need no adornment apart from being teamed with a contrasting almond green jug. Tulips are unusual in that they continue to grow and move once picked and put in water. Allow for this when you arrange them.*

Above: *Gerberas have marvelous stiff stems that stay just where you put them. Placed in a narrow-necked container, they need no other mechanics to support them and make a bold, modern statement that contrasts here with a pretty, florally decorated bedroom.*

Ringing the changes

All kinds of unlikely containers can be used to make interesting arrangements, as long as you can find a way to line them or conceal a container with water in them. Remember that a group of two or more small arrangements can make more visual impact than one on its own. Vary the heights of different containers.

Sweet simplicity

Many people are nervous about the idea of flower arranging, imagining that there are rules to keep and styles to follow. The answer is to forget all this and go for something as simple as possible. The schemes on these pages are perfect for both modern interior or period homes and will give you the confidence to try out your own ideas and variations. What they have in common is an elegance that comes from using unfussy containers and simple color schemes. Bunches of blooms used generously, but with no complicated mechanics, will provide stunning results every time.

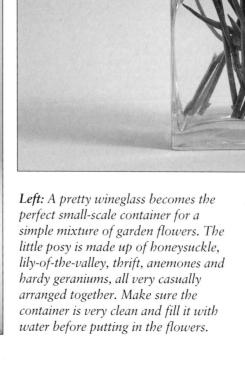

Left: A pretty wineglass becomes the perfect small-scale container for a simple mixture of garden flowers. The little posy is made up of honeysuckle, lily-of-the-valley, thrift, anemones and hardy geraniums, all very casually arranged together. Make sure the container is very clean and fill it with water before putting in the flowers.

Above: Highly scented freesias are usually available all the year round and are useful for arranging with other varieties of flower. Here, they are displayed on their own, in a simple rectangular glass vase. Keep the buds opening along the stem by removing faded and dying flowers from the bottom as they wither away.

Simply stunning

You need not always arrange flower stems individually. With sweet peas and daffodils, for example, you can take all the flowers in one hand to make a fat bunch, cut all the stems to the same length, place the whole bunch in a jug and let it drop. Loosen the flower heads a little if they seem too squashed together.

Below: *The strong simplicity of gerbera daisies calls for a bold display. Try using a simple container, such as this round glass goldfish bowl, and fill it generously. Add the blooms one at a time, working round the bowl. Finish off by adding several strands of bear grass to curve away from the edge.*

Right: *Sweet peas look their best simply displayed in a clear glass jug. The vibrant mix of strong pastel colors always works well and their scent fills the whole room.*

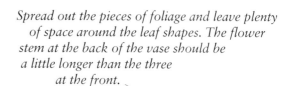

Left: The simplest elements can be made into a bold and unusual arrangement. Just five gerbera blooms and a few elegant strands of bear grass combine in a plain, round vase to stunning effect. The color scheme, too, is controlled, which gives the whole thing even more visual strength.

Below: Here, the fabulous blooms of some scented lilies have been cut short and simply displayed with one or two dahlia and chrysanthemum blooms in an interesting antique glass jello mold. Begin by placing one lily head at the side of the dish and work across the container, adding the remaining flowers. The result is an arrangement with great panache.

Spread out the pieces of foliage and leave plenty of space around the leaf shapes. The flower stem at the back of the vase should be a little longer than the three at the front.

Left: With the aid of a handful or two of clear glass marbles, you can create a dramatic arrangement with just a few dahlia blooms and some carefully chosen foliage. The marbles not only hold the stems in place, they also look decorative on their own.

Above: A bright kitchen windowsill is home to a rustic pottery jug filled with decorative garden herbs. These include variegated mint, feverfew, sage leaves, lavender, lemon balm and brilliant orange marigolds, making a fragrant and colorful arrangement. Having collected the herbs, take a few stems of each type and make them up into a small bunch. Arrange them in the vase before adding the marigolds around the edge.

Perfect posies

A tiny handful of simple wild flowers or a large bunch of glamorous blooms - however you make a posy, the results are bound to please. Posies are one of the simplest ways to arrange flowers and they make an ideal gift for all kinds of occasions. Years ago, these little bunches were known as tussie-mussies and were carried as a protection against disease and to mask unpleasant smells. Traditionally, posies are carried by a bride and her attendants and in Victorian times were given as love tokens and taken to grand balls and parties as decoration for beautiful gowns. A well-made posy (see pages 90-91) can be stood in water as a ready-made flower arrangement.

Above: *This delightful posy would be perfect for a small bridesmaid. Start by cutting into the center of a paper doily and cut a small circle out of the middle. Make a hand-held posy of mixed flowers and tie the stems tightly with wire, thread or a rubber band. Wrap the doily around the flowers, making a cone shape, then slightly overlap the cut edges of the doily and secure them with a paper clip. This posy contains annual gypsophila, lime green Alchemilla mollis and Doris pinks.*

Left: *Red, yellow and veined roses with annual gypsophila make a striking posy.*

Making a herb posy

Little posies of fresh garden herbs make the most delightful gifts or instant bouquets. Collect several different varieties of herb from the garden, including some that are in flower. Make a hand-held posy and trim the stems to the same length. Put a rubber band round the stems to hold them in place and then tie a ribbon or some decorative tape around the rubber band. If it is a gift, attach a label, too. Several such bunches would look attractive in a small basket or bowl in the kitchen and might provide inspiration and delicious fresh ingredients for a keen cook.

Right: *It takes very little time to create small posies from garden flowers. Years ago, these little tussie-mussies were carried to mask unpleasant smells, which explains the presence of sweet peas and variegated mint, along with the anemones, in this little posy.*

Below: *An orange-gold ranunculus lies at the heart of this charming spring posy. It is surrounded by sprigs of scented white lilac interspersed with Narcissus 'Cheerfulness' and an outer ring of salmon-coral chrysanthemums.*

Above: *Deep pinks and reds combine to make a beautiful, richly colored posy. The dusky reddish leaves of purple sage set off the pelargonium flowers, spikes of polygonum, fuchsia flowers and delicate astrantia blooms.*

Below: *Finishing touches for posies can include decorative ribbon in a complementary or contrasting color, any kind of decorative leaves, or a paper doily frill or collar.*

Clever centerpieces

Good food deserves beautiful flowers to set the scene. A dining table, whether set for a quick breakfast or a leisurely dinner, looks finished and inviting with some kind of flower centerpiece. You can choose flowers to complement or contrast with the food, to echo a color in the plates or table linen, or simply to work within the whole room. Bear in mind that people need space to eat and should be able to see and talk easily to other guests. Keep centerpieces fairly low and though fragrant flowers are pleasing, choose nothing too scented that might clash with the food. And why not introduce flowers on informal occasions, too? A simple supper or breakfast tray can be transformed with the addition of a few carefully chosen blooms in a tumbler, cup-and-saucer or even an egg cup.

Left: An elegant arrangement on a low, stemmed fruit dish. The sweetness of so much pink is counteracted by the deeper tones of the Stargazer lilies and the touches of pale blue from the brodiaea. Put the stems in a block of damp foam taped to the dish.

Below: A quick and simple idea for a table centerpiece is to arrange some colorful fruit or vegetables and scatter a few flower heads among them. These brightly colored sweet peppers make the base for some golden-yellow chrysanthemums.

Left: *A prettily speckled summer squash has been hollowed out to hold a bunch of summer annuals. As long as you leave a certain thickness of fruit inside the skin, a squash is quite waterproof and makes an excellent flower container. Stand it on a mat or plate to avoid staining the furniture.*

Below: *A romantic outdoor dinner needs special flowers to complete the summer theme. Here, a tall glass goblet is simply filled with several different varieties of richly colored, strongly perfumed, old-fashioned garden roses. Trim off the rose thorns and leaves and cut the stems at a slant.*

Above: *A simple iced sponge cake has its own flower arrangement, which is designed in this case to look pretty but not to be eaten. Wait until the cake icing has set and is hard enough to put flowers on. Stand the cake on a plate and cut the flower stems, leaving just the heads for decoration. Lay the flowers in a circle round the edge of the plate. The jugful of garden flowers combines the rich summer color of cornflowers, sweet peas and roses.*

A vegetable 'vase'

As well as squashes, melons and pumpkins, you could use an ornamental cabbage as the focus of an unusual table decoration. As it only has to last a short time, simply cut the flower stems quite short and tuck them in amongst the layers of leaves.

Special occasions

There are often times when flower arrangements need to be spectacular. You might want to decorate the house for a party or celebration, a homecoming or anniversary, or for one of the traditional festivals that most of us celebrate at some time during the year. This is a time to be a bit more extravagant than usual and to attempt decorations on a larger scale, perhaps. It is certainly true that some 'special occasion' displays can use a great deal of plant material, but it may be enough just to choose a bigger container than normal and to select larger and more formal flowers. Alternatively, color could be the key to making something showstopping without spending more money or time than you might for an everyday display. The arrangements will depend on whether your celebration focuses around a dining or buffet table, or whether you are having a gathering of people standing in one room or using the whole house. Consider such practical points first and then plan where to put the flowers so that they make the maximum impact on your family and friends.

Pedestal displays

There are many different styles of ready-made pedestals, both modern and traditional, and there is no reason why you should not use a tall table or plant stand in place of a pedestal. Whichever you choose, make sure that the pedestal is heavy and firm, so that there is no risk of the flowers falling over. Make use of the height of a pedestal by arranging the flower stems so that they curve downwards, rather than in a stiff, upward outline. Be sure to tape the container or block of flower foam securely to the top of the pedestal and try to keep the center of gravity of the plant arrangement low.

Right: A small porcelain bowl is filled with a mixture of apricot and peach flowers to decorate a guest bedroom windowsill. Several small posies or displays look more welcoming than one large arrangement in guest rooms.

Above: A fabulous mixture of dozens of different flowers is like a glorious celebration of summer. Many of the flowers are garden grown, while others are more exotic and available only from the florist. This large-scale arrangement would make a stunning focal point in a room to be used for a party or celebration.

Right: A rich textural arrangement of summer flowers in a classic urn-shaped vase. A square of crumpled wire over floral foam in the neck of the container helps to support the long and top-heavy stems of larkspur, lilac, delphiniums, stocks and aquilegia.

Above: In winter, when flowers are scarce, make use of glossy evergreen foliage and luscious fruit to create a spectacular table centerpiece for a party, special occasion or during Christmas festivities.

Above: Always begin a pedestal arrangement by setting the size and outline with solid shapes of foliage or filler material. Fill in with more long-stemmed plants, bringing plenty out towards the front. Finally, add the important blooms and smaller material to create a balanced, well-filled effect. Here, gerbera, genista and antirrhinum make a superb spring mixture.

Garlands and wreaths

In recent years, we have become used to seeing garlands and wreaths at all times of the year. At one time, circlets of evergreens were commonly used to decorate houses at Christmas, but now there are few occasions when wreaths and garlands would not fit in. You can use fresh or dried flowers of all kinds and there is a choice of frames on which to base your arrangement. A wreath can be made on a damp foam or moss base, or you can attach dried flowers to foam or twig rings. A wire circle around the brim of a straw hat hanging on a wall makes an unusual base. You can put together quick and easy wreaths on a ring of woven vine branches or just on wire. Imagination is the only limitation.

Short-stemmed, fresh flowers will last for several days tucked into a damp, foam wreath base. Soak the foam first in a large bowl or sink; follow the manufacturer's guidelines.

Above: *Marigolds and nasturtiums, both culinary flowers, are combined with* Alchemilla mollis *to make this delightful garland. Golden marjoram leaves add a sweet herbal scent.*

Covering frames

One way of covering a wire frame is to wrap moss all round it, securing the moss with thin rose wire. (You can buy this by the reel.) Add the flowers and leaves, pushing the short stems into the moss and securing them with more wire if necessary. Spray the completed garland with water to keep it fresh.

Another approach is to cover the frame completely with leaves or filler material. Add single flowers of the same type at regular intervals right round the frame. Finish off by filling in the spaces between the main flowers with other small flowers or even little bunches of blooms.

Above: *White hydrangeas, scented jasmine, sweet peas and veronica all feature in this cool, sparkling display of late summer garden blooms. The background is made up of steely blue rue foliage. (Handle rue with care; the juice from the stems can irritate skin that is later exposed to sunlight.)*

Above: *A light and bright summer garland made from daisies, jasmine, feverfew, cornflowers, variegated mint leaves, love-in-a-mist and golden-yellow achillea. Strong flowers always look fresh if they are mixed with plenty of white for contrast.*

Right: *This frothy wreath is made with a base of Alchemilla mollis. Tucked in amongst this are small, purple hardy geranium flowers and sweet peas. Tiny pieces of green sedum and stokesia flowers complete the picture.*

Finish off a sumptuous garland such as this with a generous ribbon in a complementary pastel color.

181

Beautiful baskets

Baskets have always seemed a natural and highly suitable container to present flowers in. The subtle browns and beiges and interesting textures of the vast range now available, from rough and twisted to smooth and glossy, make a perfect background to the delicate petals and glowing colors of flowers and foliage. If you intend to use a basket for fresh flowers that need water, then you will have to use a plastic liner or inner container, or take advantage of the easy-to-use floral foams, which are ideal for this particular method of display.

Above: A heart-shaped basket is ideal for a Valentine's Day gift. Here, single white daisies, scented white lilac and apricot carnations have been arranged around golden yellow rosebuds.

Above: A pretty handled basket needs the simplest treatment to show it off best. Here, pink and white hyacinths are combined generously and arranged in a mass of glossy, dark green, evergreen ivy leaves. The soft, gentle scent is very evocative of spring.

Left: A basket like this is easy to make if you follow a few simple guidelines. First cut the foam to fit the lined container, then soak it and fit it into place before packing the flowers in closely together, working from the pointed end outwards. Allow some of the flowers to hang slightly over the edges. Choose the flowers and colors with care; here, aquilegias, saxifrage, pelargoniums, chive blooms and pale anemones combine to great effect.

182

Below: Woven, stained natural wood and bright plastic combine to make a pretty basket which, filled with flowers, makes an ideal gift for any occasion. The tall handle makes it easy to carry. Choose simple flowers, such as single daisies and spray carnations, to echo the style of the basket. Add a ribbon for decoration.

Right: A finely woven, glossy basket in a rich toffee brown is the perfect foil for spikes of deep purple Iris reticulata. Buy them as small pot plants and remove them from their pots before packing them quite close together in the lined basket. Disguise the potting mix and the base of the stems with moss for a natural look.

Below: This flat basket is ideal for a dried flower arrangement in a strong color scheme of orange and yellow. Cut short the foliage and flower stems and glue them into place, preferably with a glue gun.

Index to Plants

Credits

The majority of the photographs featured in this book have been taken by Neil Sutherland and are © Colour Library Books. The publishers wish to thank the following photographers for providing additional photographs, credited here by page number and position on the page, i.e. (B)Bottom, (T)Top, (C)Center, (BL)Bottom left, etc.

A-Z Botanical Photographic Collection: Michael R. Chandler 24(B)
Pat Brindley: 38(TR), 47(BR)
Eric Crichton: 24(T), 28-29(B), 37(CL, BL), 46, 47(TR), 48(T), 53(TL), 71(T), 72(BL)
John Glover: Copyright page, 19(BR), 25(L, CR), 28(L), 29(T), 34(R), 35(BL), 40(TR),
44, 44-45(T),
45, 53(R), 57(BR), 65(TR)
Natural Image: Bob Gibbons 52(L), 68(C), Liz Gibbons 52(BR)
Clive Nichols: 10(L), 14, 15 (Keukenhof Gardens), 23(CT, Designer Jill Billington),
25(BR), 28(TR), 29(R), 30(L), 31(TL, TC, TR), 33(BC, BR), 35(TR, BR), 36(L), 39(TL,
TR), 40(BL), 41(CT, B), 42(BR), 47(L, Designer Wendy Francis), 48(BL), 48-49(B),
49(TL, R), 52(TR), 55(TL, TR, BR), 62(TL),
63(TL, TR), 66(TR), 68-69(C), 69(BL, BR, CR), 70(B)
Photos Horticultural: 53(B), 57(TL)
Daan Smit: 35(TL)
Harry Smith Photographic Collection: 39(BR), 41(TR), 70(TR), 71(CB)
Don Wildridge: 34(BL)

Acknowledgments

The publishers would like to thank Country Gardens at Chichester for providing plants and photographic facilities for the first part of this book; thanks are particularly due to Cherry Burton and Sue Davey for their enthusiastic help and guidance.